GUIDANCE MONOGRAPH SERIES

Shelley C. Stone

Bruce Shertzer

Editors

GUIDANCE MONOGRAPH SERIES

The general purpose of Houghton Mifflin's Guidance Monograph Series is to provide high quality coverage of topics which are of abiding importance in contemporary counseling and guidance practice. In a rapidly expanding field of endeavor, change and innovation are inevitably present. A trend accompanying such growth is greater and greater specialization. Specialization results in an increased demand for materials which reflect current modifications in guidance practice while simultaneously treating the field in greater depth and detail than commonly found in textbooks and brief journal articles.

The list of eminent contributors to this series assures the reader expert treatment of the areas covered. The monographs are designed for consumers with varying familiarity to the counseling and guidance field. The editors believe that the series will be useful to experienced practitioners as well as beginning students. While these groups may use the monographs with somewhat different goals in mind, both will benefit from the treatment given to content areas.

The content areas treated have been selected because of specific criteria. Among them are timeliness, practicality, and persistency of the issues involved. Above all, the editors have attempted to select topics which are of major substantive concern to counseling and guidance personnel.

Shelley C. Stone

Bruce Shertzer

THE MENTALLY RETARDED STUDENT AND GUIDANCE

EARL J. HEATH

PURDUE UNIVERSITY

HOUGHTON MIFFLIN COMPANY · BOSTON

NEW YORK · ATLANTA · GENEVA, ILL. · DALLAS · PALO ALTO

TO HIRAM AND ELMA HEATH,
AND HENRY AND NETTIE NEEDHAM,
WHO TAUGHT ME MUCH ABOUT LIFE.
TO MY WIFE BETTY,
DAUGHTER DIANNE, AND SON EARL J,
WHO CONTINUALLY ADD TO MY EDUCATION.

CONTENTS

EDITORS' INTRODUCTION

Historically, school counselors have not been involved to any great extent with retarded children in the schools. Many factors have contributed to this condition and will continue to do so. Not the least among these is the hard fact that relatively few mentally retarded individuals receive much schooling, even in special education programs. Compounding the lack of programs for the retarded are the parallel facts that 1) most such programs exist at the elementary school level, and 2) counseling services have been concentrated at the secondary school level in American education. For these reasons and others, school counselors rarely come into contact with retarded youth, and consequently, have had little opportunity to use knowledge of these individuals and to provide services to them.

Increasing attention at the national, state, and local level has been devoted to the mentally retarded in the United States during the decade of the sixties. Concern and interest have increased and, perhaps more importantly, both material and monetary support have been provided. All of this promises much in the way of improved identification, treatment, and education of this segment of our population. While these moves are badly needed and represent an improvement, much remains to be done.

In this monograph Professor Heath presents an overview of the field of mental retardation: its terminology, diagnostic procedures, educational programs, and vocational planning and placement. The sample material presented in the appendices will undoubtedly be useful to individuals who wish to become aware of the scope of services available within a typical state. The descriptions and materials presented from functioning model programs portray realistically and clearly the activities and services available in specialized non-school agencies.

We believe that this monograph will be helpful to counselors not only because of its content but also because of the challenge it presents to those who work in the helping professions. Whether or not the counselor agrees with the specific ways in which Professor Heath views the school counselor's function with retarded students, he cannot escape the increasing probability that in some form his services are sorely needed by these children.

SHELLEY C. STONE

BRUCE SHERTZER

AUTHOR'S INTRODUCTION

Vocational guidance for the mentally retarded student cannot wait until he reaches the age of fifteen or sixteen and becomes a candidate for services by the Vocational Rehabilitation Counselor. It must be begun very early in life in the home and followed throughout all of his school years if he is to develop the proper attitude toward work, good work habits, and skills.

The special education programs need the services and skills of the school counselor to provide a well-rounded program. There is a role for the counselor in the elementary school with the retarded student. This role increases in scope with each year the retardate is in school. The school-work study program for the retarded will be successful to the degree the counselor works with the special education teacher in preparing the students, and with the Rehabilitation Counselor and the community in "selling" the "employer-trainers" on the important role they can play in helping the retarded find a useful life.

The author was asked to write *The Mentally Retarded Student and Guidance* as a handbook to provide a brief introduction for counselors to the retarded students they meet or will be meeting in their schools. Some suggestions are made as to appropriate roles the counselor can play in working with the special education program to bring about a more adequate program. Challenges are issued to the counselor to join in the applied research needed to bring about a revolution in the rehabilitation of the retarded.

Many people have contributed much to the preparation of this monograph and wherever possible their contribution has been acknowledged in the book. Some of those whose contributions cannot be adequately recognized include:

Dr. Joseph Hollis and Dr. Louis Schmidt, who helped the author develop a basic philosophy of guidance through their teaching.

Dr. M. C. Beyerl, who has been the author's close friend, confidant, and consultant in the area of vocational rehabilitation of the mentally retarded for many years. He has been responsible, more than any other, for helping the author develop a basic philosophy of life.

Mr. Demos Gallendar, Administrator of Ginsberg Rehabilitation Center at Fort Wayne State Hospital and Training Center, who contributed much of the current material on the Ginsberg Rehabilitation Center and who read the manuscript, offering valuable suggestions to the author.

Mr. James Tilton, Executive Director of Wabash Center for the Mentally Retarded, who contributed the material on the Wabash Center facilities and program.

Mr. Paul Lane, Director of Special Education in the Lafayette Indiana School Corporation, for his continuous cooperation and his dialogue with the author regarding the cooperative role between the counselor and the special educators.

Mrs. Sara Cochran, Mrs. Kaaren Jessen, and Miss Valerie Cotner, my students and assistants, for their contributions to the content of the monograph.

Mrs. Carla Barcus and Mrs. Diana Kelley, for their tremendous efforts in preparing and typing the manuscript.

Earl J. Heath

1

Philosophy of Education and Guidance for the Mentally Retarded

Of all children in the world, perhaps none is more discriminated against than the handicapped. If the handicapped child is also mentally retarded, the discrimination may become even more intense.

Our society with its heavy emphasis on competition at every level tends to frown on those not as well equipped to compete in life's arena. The advanced technological age into which we are rapidly moving in all phases of life adds heavily to the inadequacies of the retarded. It becomes increasingly easy to look at the retarded as less than human. Thus, any special arrangements for their education, vocational training, special placement, and health may be looked upon as an "act of charity" by many educators, as well as by society in general.

The birth of an obviously retarded child arouses serious emotional reactions from parents, family, and friends. Parents usually experience guilt feelings that sometimes require extended professional help to allay. Many feel that this is God's punishment for some personal sin in their life. Some physicians advise parents that they should try to get their retarded child admitted to a state school for the retarded or other institution as soon as possible. Some physicians cannot respond to the

1

parents' distress because of their own emotional "hangups" or simply because they do not wish to take the time to get involved.

Thus, the retarded child enters an already hostile environment that has been made more so by the anxieties and insecurities of those who should be protecting him and building his security.

In addition to those children who are obviously retarded at birth, there are many children whose retardation is not recognized until later, perhaps not until they begin school. They are looked upon as "slow-developers" who will "outgrow this problem." We are learning to recognize these children at an early age and are developing programs that begun early, will help them reach their maximum potential.

The emotional impact of the identification of the retarded child extends far beyond the immediate circle of family, friends, and family physician. The church, the various welfare agencies, the schools, and the taxpayers also react, usually negatively, at the thought of another problem child. The taxpayer will be forced to dig a little deeper into his already over-burdened wallet to provide funds for the expansion of programs he does not understand and from which he feels he will not even remotely benefit. Few of these individuals understand or accept the often repeated philosophy that our concern must be to assist the mentally retarded to become taxpayers rather than tax-consumers.

Children who function intellectually and socially at a retarded level have been with us since the beginning of time and will more than likely be present in increasing numbers for many years to come. Several reasons for this probable increase include:

1. *Population growth.* The ratio of mentally retarded will remain approximately the same, but the total number of such children will increase at a proportionate rate to the growth of the population.

2. *Advances in medical science.* The average life span continues to be lengthened because of ever-increasing knowledge in medical fields. The development of new drugs for controlling disease and significant techniques for repair or replacement of damaged or diseased organs has resulted in a normal life span for children who previously would not have survived. Though much has been done to keep the organism alive, much remains to be done to prevent original insults to the organism and to eliminate the residual effects of these insults. As a result, the child lives longer, but continues to function at a retarded level.

3. *More accurate identification of the mentally retarded.* As more special education programs for the retarded become available in the public schools, greater emphasis will be given to identifying children who need these services. The better the program and the more suc-

cessful the program is in dealing with the problems of retarded children, the less resistance the school will receive from parents when placing children in special programs designed to help them learn.

4. *Earlier identification of handicapped children.* Kephart (1968) describes two surveys which indicate that between 15 and 20 percent of all children in the public schools have learning disabilities. Many children so classified are functionally retarded.

Dillon, Heath, and Biggs (1970) found that when children with learning disabilities are identified early in life and special, developmentally based training programs are established for them, the majority can close the educational gap between them and their peers. In their study of 150 students screened from approximately 1,000 incoming first-grade students and identified as children likely to fail in school, a mean IQ increase of 21.7 points was obtained the first year. On the pre-test of the Otis Mental Ability Test, 25 children scored 75 or below; whereas, on the post-test at the end of the first grade only one child received an IQ score below 75. The retention rate in the first grade dropped from 10.8% the previous year to 1.49% for those children not included in the experimental group the first year of the experiment. This indicated that the majority of the children in the study were functionally retarded in the academic setting. A developmentally based curriculum was constructed that allowed the child to enter academic studies when he was ready to do so. At the middle of the second year of the project, most of the children in the experimental group were classified as readers, though many problems remained to be worked out. This project is a longitudinal, action research study supported by a Title III grant.

Since the beginning of the twentieth century, there has been a deepening appreciation of the dignity of all men and a better understanding of the interrelatedness of the individuals who comprise our culture. Out of this awareness has come an increasing concern for the well-being of the children in our society. While the major implementation of this concern has been directed towards children who are "normal," a constantly increasing amount of attention has been directed towards solving the problems of groups of children with specific handicaps.

Much had been done to improve the lot of the mentally retarded in previous years; however, major attention was focused on their needs on October 17, 1961. On this date, President John F. Kennedy appointed the President's Panel on Mental Retardation and charged them with the exploration of all aspects of mental retardation and the preparation of a comprehensive and long-range plan for dealing with the crucial problems. Six separate task forces were organized to deal with the problems of prevention, education and rehabilitation, law and public awareness, biological research, behavioral and social research, and coordination. Their report was published in October, 1962.

The Panel's report (1962) cited many revealing statistical findings related to the enormity and intensity of the problems associated with mental retardation. A summary of these findings follows:

1. There were approximately five and one-half million mentally retarded in the United States. By 1970, the Panel estimated there would be approximately one million more, with 126,000 mentally retarded babies being born each year.

2. Only 400,000 of the mentally retarded require constant care and supervision while the other five million are only mildly handicapped.

3. Fifteen to twenty million people live in families with a retarded child. Thus, mental retardation is a serious problem to one out of twelve people. Ninety-six percent of all mentally retarded persons live in private homes.

4. Over 200,000 mentally retarded are cared for in public institutions at a cost to state and local taxpayers of over three hundred million dollars per year.

5. Each year, over 250 million dollars are spent on special education and other benefits by state and local groups. The federal government spends an additional 164 million dollars on the mentally retarded.

6. Four percent of all persons examined for induction in the armed forces during World War II were mentally retarded.

7. One of four beds in mental institutions is occupied by a mentally retarded patient. The average state hospital has 367 more patients than its rated capacity with an average waiting list of 340 individuals per hospital.

8. Mental retardation disables *twice* as many persons as blindness, polio, cerebral palsy, and heart disease *combined; ten times* as many as diabetes; *twenty times* as many as muscular dystrophy; and *six hundred times* as many as infantile paralysis.

9. Only mental illness, cardiac disease, arthritis, and cancer have a higher prevalence than mental retardation and all of these conditions usually occur late in life.

President Kennedy's charge to the Panel is essential reading for all persons interested in the mentally retarded. He demonstrates a dynamic grasp of the problems of the mentally retarded, probably growing out of personal knowledge and experience. A portion of his speech revealing the heart of his challenge follows:

Much of the world's population still struggles for mere survival; others for domination of the weaker. Our aim is national and individual dignity. Our fortune is scientific and technological ability. Our obligation is to search for the secrets of the human mind and to share our knowledge throughout the world.

Discoveries of the wheel, the internal combustion engine, and principles of thermodynamics have liberated mankind from much physical labor. Two hundred years ago man demonstrated through the discoveries of Lavoisier and Harvey that human life is governed by universal physical laws. Major progress in science and medicine can be measured from that date. Until the last two decades, however, little research was concentrated on the nature of the living cell and its reproduction. But great strides have been made in that direction through the understanding of the chemical basis of genes and chromosomes and their governing role in life itself.

The future belongs to those who carry forward these achievements. It is now possible to attack the causes and prevention, as well as the treatment, of mental retardation. This will require new breakthroughs, but it will pay enormous dividends in knowledge about ourselves, for the functions of the brain represent an almost completely uncharted frontier. The basic research entailed in such an effort will prove the essence of human development, and its results may far exceed its objectives. Exploration and discovery in this field may uncover the secrets of life and man's capacities, and the answer to many mysteries of social behavior. Perhaps even more important, an understanding of the motivation and effect of human behavior offers the hope of fostering the rational behavior of nations.

Progress in the natural sciences during the past fifteen years has been impressive, but achievements in the prevention and therapy of mental retardation can be even more spectacular and can bring important benefits to mankind.

President Kennedy's public acknowledgement that his sister was mentally retarded and later the introduction of Vice-President Hubert Humphrey's retarded granddaughter to the public did much to remove the stigma from families with retarded children.

Brief History of Education of the Mentally Retarded

The severely retarded have been recognized since the earliest days of civilization. They presented socio-economic problems that were resolved in the harsh manner of the times. The Spartans and the Greeks practiced abandonment of "idiots" or cast them into rivers to drown. Abandonment was also practiced in England and Rome and other parts of the then civilized world.

The word "idiot" is derived from the Greek term "Iditos" or "idios". This means a person set apart or alone and implies that the mentally retarded live in a world by themselves more or less outside the realm of society. Since the most ancient recorded history the retarded have been treated as grossly different from other citizens of their day. Extreme strategies have been applied to them which range from ostracism, persecution, and neglect to reverence. They have been considered incapable of human feelings and undeserving of any human compassion or consideration.

Christ's example and teaching on duty toward the weak and helpless eventually brought some relief to the mentally retarded. Since the time of Christ there are records of numerous instances of a growing recognition of the moral and social responsibility of society for the care of the mentally retarded. Legend states that the Bishop of Mym, later known as Saint Nicholas, demonstrated compassion toward the retarded in the fourth century.

In the sixteenth century, Saint Vincent de Paul and his Sisters of Charity established the first public institution in Paris, the Bicerte. Here, they cared for the mentally retarded along with other handicapped persons.

During the middle ages the mentally retarded received homage in certain localities because of the superstitious belief that they were children of the Divine. They frequently served as court fools and jesters, earning the favor and support of the royalty. However, as late as the Reformation, certain religious groups still regarded the mentally retarded as being filled with Satan and dealt harshly with them. American Indians thought of the retarded as being "children of the Great Spirit" and allowed them to live freely in the villages.

Educational programs for the mentally retarded did not come into being until the nineteenth century. Jean Marc Gaspard Itard, a member of the medical staff of the institution for the deaf-mutes of Paris and a philosopher, made the first scientific attempt to educate a retarded person.

A wild boy had been captured by some hunters near Avignon in 1799 at the age of eleven or twelve. He was found naked in the woods living on acorns and roots for food. He was wild in appearance and unable to speak. Study indicated that he selected his food by smell and that he could not distinguish between hot and cold. The conclusion was reached that this child who was more animal-like than human was an incurable idiot.

Itard did not agree and set out to civilize the boy whom he named Victor. He attempted to teach him to speak and to use his senses and intelligence to learn. Itard worked with Victor for a five-year period, gradually coming to the conclusion that the boy was mentally defective. He changed his educational methods and was able to teach him many things. Though Victor never learned to speak, he learned to read and write many words and was able to exchange simple written communications with other people.

With the onset of Victor's puberty Itard had to abandon his work because the boy became uncontrollable. Victor spent the rest of his life in custodial care, and died at approximately forty years of age.

Itard considered his experiment a failure. However, after some years had passed, the French Academy of Science, recognizing the significance of his work, prevailed upon him to record his experiment. His book, *The Wild Boy of Avignon*, is still considered a classic for educators of the mentally retarded. Due to Itard's work, major reforms in the treatment of mental defectives began to be made throughout the civilized world. Itard first demonstrated that the severely mentally retarded would respond to training though only minimal results might be expected. His work led to the stimulation of further experimentation in the area of the education of the mentally retarded and in the area of psychological principles involved in the learning process.

Edward Sequin, a medically oriented student of Itard's, published a book on his principles of education for the retarded in 1846. This book, entitled *The Moral Treatment, Hygiene and Education of Idiots and Other Backward Children,* presented his theories of educating the retarded based on a neurophysiological hypothesis. Sequin moved to the United States in 1848 where he laid the foundations for programs for the mentally retarded. His second book, published in 1866 and entitled *Idiocy: Its Treatment by the Physiological Method,* set forth his basic philosophy for educating the retarded. Many of his basic principles of educating the mentally retarded continue to be fostered in present day curriculums.

Kirk and Johnson (1951) summarize Sequin's contribution as follows: "He emphasized the education of the whole child, the individualization of instruction, the importance of rapport between teacher and pupil, the physical comfort of the child during the learning period, and the importance of beginning with what the child needs, wants and desires before progressing to areas that are unknown."

About 1897 Maria Montessori, an Italian psychiatrist, became interested in the problems of the mentally retarded because of the large number of such children in the insane asylums of Rome. After reviewing the work of Itard and Sequin she reached the conclusion that the problem was basically an educational one. She organized the Orthophrenic School for the education of the mentally retarded children and also for the training of teachers. Her work greatly influenced pre-school education in the United States as well as the education of the mentally retarded.

Decroly, a Belgian physician, concluded that the best treatment for mentally defective children was an educational program. He believed that the education program should center around the child and his needs. He is considered one of the more modern educators of mentally retarded children.

Another of the early pioneers who is considered among the first modern educators of the retarded was Alfred Binet, an experimental psychologist whose doctorate was in science rather than medicine. Binet's major concern was for the whole child and emphasized making him occupationally and socially competent. As most students know, he is better known for his contribution in the area of diagnosis of intellectual level than in the area of educational methodology.

Perhaps the person who did most to bridge the gap between the sensory and physiological approach of Itard and Sequin and the modern methods of teaching retarded children according to their needs within society, was Alice Descoeudres, a French woman. Her book, *The Education of Mentally Defective Children,* dealt with the development of a comprehensive educational program for mentally retarded children. She believed in the unit method of teaching and the individualization of instruction, and was a strong advocate of Dewey's philosophy of "learning by doing."

Educational work with the mentally retarded in America began in the early 1800's. In July, 1850, H. B. Wilbur opened a private school in Barne, Massachusetts. This was the first such school in the United States. In 1851 Massachusetts established the Massachusetts School for Idiotic and Feeble-Minded Youth. From 1850 to the early 1900's was the era of great growth of institutions for the mentally retarded. Public schools did not provide programs until the close of the nineteenth century. Providence, Rhode Island, established a class in 1896 and Springfield, Massachusetts, in 1899.

Boston hired its first teacher of mentally defective children in November, 1898, with its class actually beginning January 30, 1899, at the Appleton Street Primary School House. By 1906 Boston had seven classes for mentally defective children, with an enrollment of slightly under 100. Chicago opened its first class in the fall of 1900. By 1911, 222 cities reported classes organized for mentally defective children. By 1930 this number had risen to 354 cities. By 1948, 719 cities had classes. By 1969, almost every city, county, and town had programs for handicapped children. Despite this growth only one out of five handicapped children was receiving services.

Familiar names on the American scene in the development of educational programs for the mentally retarded include those of Wallin, Ingram, Inskeep, Howe, Kirk, Johnson, Cruickshank, Kephart, and a host of others. A more detailed history of education for the mentally retarded may be found in Kirk and Johnson (1951).

Definitions

Many definitions of mental retardation have been put forth. Each one has reflected the orientation of the definer. Recently the American Association on Mental Deficiency adopted the following definition:

> Mental Retardation refers to sub-average general intellectual functioning which originates during the developmental period and is associated with impairment in adaptive behavior. (Heber, 1961)

A proposal to modify this definition, which was intended to remove some of the objections to the language used in the definition rather than alter the fundamental concepts involved, was presented by Kidd (1964). His definition, which gives more precision to the semantics used, follows:

> Mental retardation refers to significantly sub-average intellectual functioning which manifests itself during the developmental period and is characterized by inadequacy in adaptive behavior.

Perhaps the best known and most often quoted of the older definitions is Doll's (1941), an elaboration on Tredgold's (1937) biological point of view of mental retardation. Doll's definition reads:

> The mentally deficient person is (1) socially incompetent, that is, socially inadequate and occupationally incompetent and unable to manage his own affairs; (2) mentally subnormal; (3) retarded intellectually from birth or early age; (4) retarded at maturity; (5) mentally deficient as a result of constitutional origin, through heredity or disease; and (6) essentially incurable.

Telford and Sawrey (1967) point out the three characteristics that distinguish the American Association on Mental Deficiency definition from Doll's definition:

1. The potential of the person is not suggested, rather his present intellectual functioning level is considered.

2. Cause is not considered, whereas organicity and its enduring nature was specified.

3. Neither curability nor incurability are considered. It is no longer felt that the prognosis and final outcome are essential to the definition (not that they are not important considerations in program planning).

It is important to note that the A.A.M.D. definition requires the presence of all three conditions — "sub-average intellectual functioning," "originates during the developmental period," and "impairment in adapting behavior" — for a person to be labelled mentally retarded. Thus, the definition is couched in functional terms rather than in the biological conditions of the older definitions of mental retardation. For a more detailed study of the definitions of mental retardation see Doll (1941), Kirk and Johnson (1951), Heber (1961), Blatt (1961), and Kidd (1964).

Labeling

Various labels have been applied to those persons functioning at a below average intellectual level. These include mental defectives, mentally subnormal, intellectually defective, intellectually subnormal, intellectually retarded, oligophrenic, feebleminded, amental, exceptional, slow-learner, and mentally retarded among others.

The World Health Organization and the American Psychiatric Association promote the term "mental subnormality" to cover the whole range of those functioning at an intellectual level below average. The American Association on Mental Deficiency (A.A.M.D.), though it has for the present retained the term "mental deficiency" in its name, is promoting the use of the term "mental retardation." The Council on Exceptional Children (CEC) and the National Association for Retarded Children (NARC) also promote the use of the term "mental retardation." In the United States there is little doubt that the term "mental retardation" has the most popular professional usage as the proper generic term for the mentally subnormal.

Criteria for Identification of the Mentally Retarded

The purpose of the identification of the mentally retarded must be kept in mind, since the criteria used for identification will vary greatly with the purpose. If the purpose is to determine academic potential and proper class placement, heavy emphasis will be placed on mental test scores (psychometric criteria) and upon school achievement (educational criteria). On the other hand, if the person is beyond the school age group, the criteria of social adjustment and economic self-sufficiency are much more relevant.

Research has shown that it is highly probable that the child who is classified as mentally retarded during the school years would not have been so classified prior to becoming of school age nor after passing the school years (O'Conner and Tizard [1956] and Lemkaw, Lietze, and Casper [1942]). This can be explained in part by the greater weight being given to abstract verbal facility during the school years.

As we move into an increasingly more complex, highly technical society where many of the more menial, manual, vocational tasks are automated, it is likely that the difference in identification criteria may become less pronounced. Therefore, society itself must be considered, as well as the purpose, in the diagnostic criteria for identification of the mentally retarded.

The current definitions of mental retardation discussed previously assume that the level of intellectual functioning be determined by psychometric criteria, that learning ability be determined by educational criteria, and that the social adjustment criteria be determined by the social and economic competence of the individual. If each of these categories of criteria is compatible in indicating a diagnosis of mental retardation, a fourth criterion, developmental, based on the child's anatomical, physiological, motor, and social development will add strength to the diagnosis.

A diagnosis of mental retardation can be seriously questioned, even though social and psychometric data dictate it, when there is a history of normal development and no record of physical or mental trauma.

Terminology and Classification

Table 1 indicates the various terminology that has applied to the mentally retarded.

The terminology most appropriate for consideration in this monograph includes that of the A.A.M.D. and that of the American Education system. The A.A.M.D. recommends the generic term "mental retardation" with the degree of subnormality represented by the terms *borderline, mild, moderate, severe,* and *profound.* These terms have fewer emotional overtones than the older terms of *feebleminded, moron, imbecile,* and *idiot.* Additionally, they more accurately convey the degree of impairment.

The American educational system has adopted the terminology "mental retardation" as the generic term and *educable, trainable,* and *custodial* to indicate degrees of mental retardation. This terminology provides information more for administrative placement than it does for answering questions of etiology and prognosis.

TABLE 1

Terminology Levels of Retardation and I.Q. Equivalents of Mental Retardation†

Organization	Generic Term	Levels of Retardation				
U.S. Institutions & Clinics						
Early	Feebleminded		Moron	Imbecile	Idiot	
Later	Mental Deficiency		Moron	Imbecile	Idiot	
Recent*	Mentally Retarded	Borderline	Mild	Moderate	Severe	Profound
American Association on Mental Deficiency	Mentally Retarded	Borderline	Mild	Moderate	Severe	Profound
Recommended I.Q. Equivalents	0–85	70–84	55–69	40–55	25–39	Below 25
Education Systems						
United States	Mentally Retarded		Educable	Trainable	Custodial	
I.Q. Equivalents	0–75		50–75	30–50	Below 30	
British	Amentia		Educational Subnormal	Backward		
I.Q. Equivalents	0–70		50–70	20–50	Below 20	
World Health Organization	Mental Subnormality		Mild	Moderate	Severe	
American Psychiatric Assn.	Mental Subnormality		Mild	Moderate	Severe	

† Adopted by author and simplified from Telford, C. W. and Sawrey, J. M., *The Exceptional Individual.* Englewood Cliffs: Prentice-Hall, 1967, p. 164.

* Most have accepted the recommended terminology and levels of retardation recommended by the A.A.M.D.

Table 1 also compares the approximate IQ equivalents of the British educational terminology and the recommended IQ equivalents of the American educational system. The American educational IQ equivalents are the same as the British when the terms "educable" and "educational subnormal" are equated, when "trainable" and "backward" are equated and when those below an IQ of 30 are considered "custodial."

The A.A.M.D. goes beyond the other classification systems in adding the category "borderline" with an IQ range of 70 to 84. They also subdivide those persons with IQ's of 39 and below into two groups — "severe" and "profound." The American educational system considers those below 30 as beyond the help of the schools and classifies them as custodial.

Table 2 presents Heber's (1959) "Conversion of IQ Scores According to Standard Deviation Values."

Heber has applied the "Range of Level in Standard Deviation Units" (now accepted by the A.A.M.D.) to the *Arthur Point Scale of Performance Tests* Form I; to the Revised *Stanford-Binet Tests of Intelligence* Forms L and M; to the *Wechsler-Bellevue Intelligence Scale* Forms I and II; to the *Wechsler Intelligence Scale for Children;* and to the *Wechsler Adult Intelligence Scale.* The range of level in standard deviation units range from –1.01 to –2.00 for Level V or "Borderline" Retardation of Measured Intelligence to <–5.0 for Level I or "Profound" Retardation of Measured Intelligence.

A comparison may be made of scores from other standardized intelligence tests by utilizing the standard deviation of that test. However a caution must be offered in that it remains the responsibility of the psychometrist to determine that the test used has been properly standardized on an adequate sample of the mentally retarded population and that acceptable reliability and validity data for the same sample is available.

Table 3, "Degrees of Mental Retardation," is a two-dimensional plot that illustrates the characteristics of the four levels of mental retardation (the borderline level was not included at that time) at different ages.

The U.S. Department of Health, Education and Welfare Committee on Mental Retardation (1962) adapted this table from one originally developed by Sloan and Birch (1955). The table is divided into groups with three age ranges: Pre-school age, 0–5; School age, 6–21; and adult, 21+. The four levels of retardation are represented in the rows and the ages involved are represented in the columns. The columns also indicate the major areas of functioning being assessed—"Maturation and Development," "Training and Education," and "Social and Vocational Adequacy." Each cell has descriptive terms of adaptive be-

TABLE 2

Conversion of IQ Scores According to Standard Deviation Values*

Level**	Range of Level in Standard Deviation Units	Arthur Point Scale of Performance Tests Form I	Revised Stanford-Binet Tests of Intelligence Forms L&M	Wechsler-Bellevue Intelligence Scale Forms I&II; Wechsler Intelligence Scale for Children; Wechsler Adult Intelligence Scale
V	−1.01 to −2.00	83–67	83–68	84–70
IV	−2.01 to −3.00	66–50	67–52	69–55
III	−3.01 to −4.00	49–33	51–36	54–40
II	−4.01 to −5.00	32–16	35–20	
I	<−5.0	<16	<20	

* Heber, R. "A Manual on Terminology and Classification in Mental Retardation," *American Journal on Mental Deficiency*, IXIV (1959). Monog. Suppl.
** Level V — Borderline Retardation of Measured Intelligence; Level IV — Mild Retardation of Measured Intelligence; Level III — Moderate Retardation of Measured Intelligence; Level II — Severe Retardation of Measured Intelligence; Level I — Profound Retardation of Measured Intelligence.

havior that are useful in evaluation. However, the likelihood of individuals fitting clearly in a single, specific cell when their several ability levels are assessed is relatively remote. In intelligence a child may perform at one level, in motor capacity, another, and in social behavior still another. Clinically, it is necessary to make a subjective judgement of the whole child to arrive at a meaningful differential diagnosis. Thus, Table 3 is more illustrative of groups of mentally retarded persons than of a specific individual within a group.

For more information in the area of terminology and classification and characteristics of the mentally retarded, see Telford and Sawrey (1967) and Hutt and Gibby (1965).

Incidence and Cause of Mental Retardation

At present, estimates indicate that there are approximately 6,000,000 Americans who are mentally retarded. This represents 3 percent of the general population. This percentage is usually accepted as a close estimate for the entire population. However, estimates will vary considerably from village to city and from one section of the country to another. For example, the inner city district of a large metropolis may have as much as 6 percent, while a suburb of the same city may have less than one percent who are mentally retarded.

Approximately 85 percent of those classified mentally retarded are mildly retarded or educable with IQ's between 50 and 70. The number of retarded found in this classification closely approximates the theoretical expectancy if intelligence were distributed on a normal or bell-shaped curve. However, the prevalence of those retarded with IQ's below 50 far exceeds the numbers that would be expected on a normal distribution of intelligence. Telford and Sawrey (1967) point out that disease, accident, and single genes which cause severe mental retardation account for this deviation.

There are over 200 known causes of mental retardation. These causes are both hereditary and environmental. From the turn of the century until 1930, heavy emphasis was placed on hereditary causes. Since 1930, attention has been focused on the environment as the prime determiner of intellectual attainment.

The causes of mental retardation range from a single dominant gene (which accounts for a few rare types) on one extreme, to general environmental deprivation (which accounts for many of the mildly retarded) on the other extreme.

Environmental causes of retardation are usually broken into three classes — pre-natal, natal, and post-natal. Included as pre-natal causes are physical trauma, infections (of the mother), blood incompatibility,

TABLE 3

Developmental Characteristics of the Mentally Retarded*

Degrees of Mental Retardation	Pre-School Age 0–5 Maturation and Development	School Age 6–20 Training & Education	Adult 21 and Over — Social & Vocational Adequacy
Profound I.Q. below 20	Gross retardation; minimal capacity for functioning in sensorimotor areas; needs nursing care.	Some motor development present; cannot profit from training in self-help; needs total care.	Some motor and speech development; totally incapable of self-maintenance; needs complete care and supervision.
Severe I.Q. 20–35	Poor motor development; speech is minimal; generally unable to profit from training in self-help; little or no communication skills.	Can talk or learn to communicate; can be trained in elemental health habits; cannot learn functional academic skills; profits from systematic habit training.	Can contribute partially to self-support under complete supervision; can develop self-protection skills to a minimal useful level in controlled environment.

Moderate I.Q. 36–52	Can talk or learn to communicate; poor social awareness; fair motor development; may profit from self-help; can be managed with moderate supervision.	Can learn functional academic skills to approximately 4th-grade level by late teens if given special education.	Capable of self-maintenance in unskilled or semi-skilled occupations; needs supervision and guidance when under mild social or economic stress.
Mild I.Q. 53–68	Can develop social and communication skills; minimal retardation in sensorimotor areas; rarely distinguished from normal until later age.	Can learn academic skills to approximately 6th grade level by late teens. Cannot learn general high school subjects. Needs special education particularly at secondary school age levels.	Capable of social and vocational adequacy with proper education and training. Frequently needs supervision and guidance under serious social or economic stress.

* U.S. Department of Health, Education and Welfare Committee on Mental Retardation, *Mental Retardation: Activities of U.S. Department of Health, Education and Welfare.* Washington, D.C., U.S. Govt. Printing Office, 1962, p. 77.

radioactivity (X-rays, etc.), and toxic poisoning. The natal causes include prematurity, asphyxia, and traumatic birth injury.

While many of the pre-natal and natal causes of retardation continue to operate after birth, there are other causes that primarily appear postnatally. These include traumatic brain injury, infections, diet, physical health, cultural factors, home environment, and extreme environmental deprivation. As Telford and Sawrey (1967) point out, "Mental retardation is not a unitary thing. It is not a disease. It has diverse causes and physical accompaniments and embraces a rather wide range of mental levels." (See their book for a more detailed discussion of causes of mental retardation.)

Philosophical Considerations

Many of the mentally retarded in the mild and borderline classifications are intelligent enough to know that they are not as intelligent or as rapid at learning as their peers. Consequently, this intellectual realization causes considerably more emotional involvement with more social and personal adjustments to be made by this group than confront the more, or less, intelligent.

Academic programs for the retarded are often limited in scope. The majority of the retarded will be placed in a slower track (if tracking is available), in special classes (if available), allowed to sit in a regular class where they cannot possibly compete, or denied any educational opportunities.

The person labelled mentally retarded will find his vocational opportunities are extremely limited. If he is fortunate enough to be the one out of five mentally retarded who receives some education and training he can look forward to some kind of meaningful work, though he will probably need assistance in finding and keeping employment. For the majority of the mentally retarded (4 out of 5) there will be no such future.

Socially, the mentally retarded tend to be rejected even from an early age. The higher functioning are frequently taken advantage of by their brighter peers. They are made the scapegoats for mischief in school, and in many cases set up to take the blame for some violation of the law. There are few leisure time activities the retarded can participate in without the assistance of someone else.

This is a sad commentary on the American educational system and the general public. We have long given lip service to the theory of compulsory education for every child. Unfortunately, we do not practice what we preach. Viewed nationwide, there are loopholes in our compulsory education laws that allow only one mentally retarded child out of every five to participate in any kind of educational program. Some of the mentally retarded are in state institutions, some are receiving minimal training in community sheltered workshop programs, some receive minimal education in the public schools. However the vast majority remain at home receiving no education, training, or vocational guidance.

Enlightened educators and other professional persons have been vitally concerned with this lack of educational and vocational opportunities for the retarded. The American Association on Mental Deficiency has worked for many years to better the lot of the retarded. The Council on Exceptional Children, a division of the National Education Association, has also lobbied effectively at the local, state, and national levels for more and better educational opportunities for the retarded. Many professional groups such as the American Medical Association, the American Psychological Association, and others have also been involved.

Perhaps more than anyone else, the parents of the retarded have been concerned with the lack of opportunities for their children. The National Association for Retarded Children, basically a parent organization, has been fighting at all levels for better laws to provide opportunities for their children. Since its formation in 1950, the NARC has done much to educate the public concerning the plight of the retarded. Appendix B contains a list of national organizations, both professional and parents', interested in the mentally retarded. The vocational counselor is urged to belong to at least one of these organizations to keep his skills in this area up to date.

When local schools would not provide classes for retarded children, parents banded together to provide some education and vocational training. Many of these programs have been incorporated into the public schools or have begun to receive local, state, and federal tax support to continue their operations. Yet much remains to be done.

Richard Koch, Past President of the American Association on Mental Deficiency, pointed out recently that much money, time, and effort must be spent in developing local community facilities and public school programs to care for and provide education to the vast majority of the mentally retarded.

It is possible to plan an educational program that will enable the retarded child to develop to his maximum. Such a child can benefit from education, training, and guidance even though his mental age is comparable to that of a younger, "normal" child simply because he *is* able to benefit from his experiences over the years. The fifteen year old mentally retarded child will not have picked up as much from his environmental experiences as his "normal" counterpart; however, he will have gained much more in his fifteen years than will the child with a CA of eight years, and an MA of eight years.

The educator must constantly be aware that the educational programs for the retarded child must provide planned exposure to many experiences the "normal" child picks up on his own. Heath (1966) has pointed out that field trips that are well planned, with the teacher stressing (before the trip) the things the child will see, then pointing these out while on the trip, and following up the trip with a detailed review, can add greatly to the child's experiential background. Retarded children need this type of structured exposure to their environment in order to learn to cope with even the simpler elements of the environment. Careful planning must eliminate extraneous detail in the first exposure, with follow-up visits gradually broadening the retarded child's understanding of the planned learning situation.

A vocational guidance program for the mentally retarded should not only provide opportunities for verbal exposure to various types of employment open to him, but also include opportunity for actual work experience. This provides direct, meaningful experience and assists greatly in determining interest, ability, and work attitudes.

The guidance program for the retarded child should start very early in life with the counselor working with the parent to begin the development of proper attitudes toward work, work habits, and skills. When these things are begun in the home at an early age, the child's potential as a vocationally useful member of society are greatly enhanced.

Provisions should be made in the elementary programs for retarded children to experience vocational success. The teacher should help the child understand the valuable contribution he is making to the welfare of others in carrying out such activities as dusting erasers, washing blackboards, sweeping the room, emptying the trash, running errands, and other tasks she might devise for vocational training. Retarded children, whenever possible, should be given responsible positions in the cafeteria, janitorial services, and maintenance of the school. With appropriate guidance these tasks will help the child mature, see himself as a useful member of society, and view himself as someone who has something to contribute to the welfare of his fellowman. The ability of the teacher or school counselor to help the child realize the importance of his contribution is vital to the success of such a program.

As an adjunct to both the academic and vocational programs for the retarded child, a token remuneration system could be established for all tasks the child does for the school. There are several values to be derived from this program. First, many aspects of the academic instructional program can be built around the vocationally related tasks the child is involved in. His arithmetic lesson can be more readily taught in terms of the child's earnings and their purchasing power. Reading lessons built around the child's vocational assignment and including his plans for use of his earnings will have direct personal relevance to the child. Second, the child increases his sense of worth-whileness by being a contributing member of society. This helps to lessen the tremendous sense of inferiority many retarded children develop. Third, the child has the opportunity to develop good work habits and the proper attitude toward work. The importance of these attributes toward his future success in the vocational world cannot be over-emphasized.

Too many special education programs stress the teaching of academics in a "watered-down" elementary curriculum. Many school administrators, because of their lack of knowledge of the needs of special education children or because of difficulty in finding properly trained teachers, create this situation by transfering an elementary teacher (often one about ready to retire) to the special education classroom.

It is vital to the education of the mentally retarded that proper, and often distinctly different, objectives and a curriculum based on these objectives be established. Academics must be taught from a functional usage approach if the retarded are to truly benefit. Emphasizing academic abstractions, even in simplified form, is useless and often even damaging to the retarded child.

Summary

Mental retardation is an extensive and complex problem. There are many types of mental retardation in children and infinite adaptive functioning levels within individual children. It is a condition (like height and weight) that exists as part of the total child and not a separate entity. It is not an illness, such as mental illness, consequently it cannot be "cured." Proper education and training will greatly increase the retarded child's potential for a full, happy life.

2

Assessment and Evaluation
of Mental Retardation

The assessment and evaluation of the mentally retarded are highly complex processes requiring the coordinated efforts of specialists from a number of disciplines. It is necessary to study the whole child both as an entity and as an integral part of his environment. It is also necessary to determine the many forces that have been brought to bear on the developing organism and their resulting effect.

The objectives of assessment and evaluation are to determine (1) the degree of the deficiency, (2) the causes of the mental retardation, (3) the level of functioning, (4) the assets possessed, (5) a proposed treatment program, and (6) a prognosis or prediction of outcome.

Evaluation in modern competitive society is an ever present aspect of life. While all children undergo frequent assessment of their skills, the mentally retarded child is often subjected to even more than the "normal" child. In addition to any formal evaluation made by his physician as an infant, the retarded child is subjected to constant informal assessment by over-anxious parents, siblings, relatives, and friends who do so with increasing concern in the home, on the playground, at church, and in leisure time activities.

When the child reaches school age, the formal evaluation process begins in a systematic manner. Physicians, social workers, psychologists, educational clinicians, counselors, and teachers look at the whole child in depth to determine proper placement (in special classes of the public schools, community agency programs, or institutions) and later to determine school promotions, retentions, change in placement, changes in program and/or vocational potential. (Since this monograph is primarily designed for educators, we shall consider assessment and evaluation of the higher functioning mentally retarded, primarily those with an IQ of 30 or above. However, the basic format remains the same with perhaps a shift of major interest towards physical well-being for those with IQ's below 30.)

Small school systems with inadequate funds to employ the above mentioned specialists frequently use the assessment and evaluation services offered by a facility such as the Purdue Achievement Center for Children (PACC). The PACC, jointly sponsored by the Bureau of Special Health Services of the Indiana State Board of Health and Purdue University, accepts referrals from physicians, schools, community agencies, and parents (with their family physician's approval). A description of the PACC's program follows as an example of the services an external agency can provide to the public schools. See Appendix C for referral sources for assessment and evaluation facilities and resources.

Extensive evaluation is carried out by the various members of the PACC staff. Several staffings of the child are held by the multi-disciplined team of the Center and from these comes a detailed report of the findings and recommendations. Careful consideration is given not only to the usual medical, psychological, social, and academic readiness testing, but also to the child's perceptual-motor developmental state. For children with deficiencies in the perceptual-motor areas, whose school systems do not have staff, facilities, or programs to handle these problems, a home training program is available. Under the supervision of the Center, the parents (who have received considerable training by the Center) carry out the prescribed training program.

In any event, whether assessment and evaluation are done by the public school staff, a community agency, or a special achievement center, it involves much more than the administration of psychological and educational readiness tests. It is an intricate process requiring a careful gathering of information in the following areas:

1. Personal developmental data.
2. Physical health.
3. Psychological evaluation of intellectual abilities and personality characteristics.
4. Perceptual-motor development.
5. Educational or academic assessment.

Since assessment and evaluation are on-going activities and dependent upon the age of the child, vocational evaluation and estimations of the use of leisure time are added when appropriate. Each of these major areas shall be discussed in order.

Personal Developmental Data

The proper starting point for a complete assessment and evaluation of a mentally retarded child is with his personal developmental history. If the child has been under continuous medical care, much of this information can be obtained from his family physician. However, since most of the retarded come from homes that do not have continuous medical care, the school physician, social worker, counselor, or school nurse, should obtain pre-natal, natal, and post-natal data. Information such as illnesses of the mother prior to birth of the child, the birth process, the on-set of developmental activities such as crawling, walking, speaking, and dentition, childhood illnesses, accidents, surgery, and other pertinent data should be obtained.

A complete social case history is needed. This includes parental and sibling attitudes towards the retarded child and how these are manifested in the home, the social and emotional strengths and weaknesses of important members in the child's home, the economic stability of the family, the characteristics of the neighborhood, and the child's adjustment to the events and people that surround him.

Physical Health

A complete and current physical examination of the retarded child must be obtained. This may be done by the school physician or by the family physician. It is the author's opinion that all physical examinations of handicapped children for assessment and evaluation purposes should be made by the school physician, who is a vital member of the multi-discipline team. He should be present at all staffings when a differential diagnosis is made and when treatment and program plans are made.

The school physician may feel that services of other medical specialists are essential for total medical assessment. A neurologist should determine possible central nervous system damage. If seizures are present, a brain wave study should be done on an electroencephalograph (E.E.G.). Abnormal brain wave patterns may require X-rays to help determine their causes. Of course, no examination would be complete without the services of a pathologist for laboratory examinations. Other specialists should be available as needed.

Psychological Evaluation of Intellect and Personality

The assessment of the mentally retarded child's psychological characteristics will include both standardized testing and clinical evaluations of the child's functioning level in several important areas. These include (1) intellectual abilities, (2) personality characteristics, (3) academic readiness, (4) vocational interests, and (5) overall adjustment evaluation.

The psychological testing is normally done by the school psychologist or psychometrist. However, in school systems which do not employ either, the psychological testing of the mentally retarded may become the responsibility of the school counselor, the director of special education, or even a special education teacher. The extent and kind of psychological testing conducted will of course depend upon the training and competence of the examiner.

Since volumes have been written and formal courses are required in this area for school counselors, the author does not feel it necessary to explore the subject further. Suffice it to say the psychological evaluation is absolutely essential to a total assessment of the retarded child.

Perceptual-Motor Development

Few school systems are fortunate enough to have an educational clinician trained in the area of perceptual-motor assessment and evaluation. However, no assessment of a retarded child can be considered complete without a perceptual-motor evaluation. More and more studies are demonstrating the importance of motor and perceptual development to the academic success of all children. This is particularly true of the mentally retarded.

Roach and Kephart (1966) have developed the *Purdue Perceptual Motor Survey* as a clinical instrument to aid the classroom teacher to understand better the motor development needs of her charges. In the hands of a trained clinician, much can be learned about the child's state of motor perceptual development and readiness for learning.

Straus, Lehtinen, Kephart, Frostig, Kirk, Piaget, Cruickshank, Barsch, and others have pioneered in this field of assessment and training. Much remains to be done before we fully understand the implications for the "normal" as well as for the mentally retarded child in this area.

For additional information in the area of learning disabilities see Strauss and Lehtinen (1947), Kephart (1960, 1968), Roach and Kephart (1962, 1966), Frostig (1964), and Cruickshank (1961), among others. (See especially Anderson of this Series.)

Educational Assessment and Evaluation

The information to be gained from the educational assessment will vary according to the age and functioning level of the child, and the purpose of the evaluation. If the evaluation is for initial school placement, the child's readiness for academic work, linguistic skills, level of self-help skills, methods of communicating, social skills, and physical abilities should be carefully explored.

For the older, higher functioning child being considered for change of program, an in-depth assessment of his level of academic attainment must be made in addition to considering the above listed areas. Consideration must be given to the question, "Is his level of academic achievement appropriate for his intellectual abilities and the opportunities he has for learning?" The child's strengths and weaknesses must be detailed and his potential in each area determined. An estimate of the child's highest academic potential should be made though it should be carefully pointed out that this is only a best estimate and that the child may reach a much higher level or never reach the predicted level.

The educational assessment could be made by one of several educational specialists including the educational clinician who conducted the perceptual-motor assessment, a school psychologist, the special educator, or the school counselor. Another specialist who should be involved in the educational assessment is the speech and hearing therapist. If this person is also trained in language development, he can assess the child's development in this very important area.

Additional Considerations in Assessment and Evaluation for the Older Mentally Retarded Child

Assessment and evaluation for the mentally retarded must be considered a continuous process. Each of the above discussed areas will continue to be considered with each succeeding evaluation; however, the areas most intensely investigated will gradually shift to the child's developing educational, social, and vocational abilities. Leisure time usage will become an important item for consideration.

Vocational Assessment and Evaluation

Over the past 15 years that the author has been involved in vocational assessment, training, and placement of the mentally retarded, there has been a remarkable change in the approach to and sophistication in the level of assessment and evaluation. From essentially trial and error vocational placement based on rather crude evaluation techniques, sophisticated evaluation procedures and techniques have evolved that lead to more adequate vocational training and placement. Unfortunately, the majority of the retarded are denied these advantages as there are not sufficient specialized vocational evaluation and training facilities, trained vocational specialists, nor adequate vocational work study programs in the public schools. Perhaps the greatest shortage lies in the area of personnel with adequate training and experience to implement these newer, more sophisticated techniques of vocational assessment and evaluation. The following information regarding the development of an educational-vocational assessment, evaluation, and training facility, and programs giving sequencing, planning, and developing information is for those who might wish to duplicate this program.

In 1962 while serving as Director of Training at Fort Wayne State Hospital and Training Center (FWSH & TC), the author and his staff began planning a vocational rehabilitation facility at the Training Center. This facility would provide for the intensive assessment and evaluation of the vocational potential and provide intensive vocational training for the mentally retarded in the State of Indiana. Heath (1962) submitted a proposal under the Hill-Burton Act with the strong support of Bernard Dolnick, the Superintendent, Mr. H. T. Dean,[1] the Assistant Superintendent for Administration, Dr. S. T. Ginsberg, the then Commissioner of the Indiana Department of Mental Health, the Indiana Rehabilitation Planning Commission, and the Indiana General Assembly; it was funded for over $250,000 with matching funds provided by the state of Indiana of over $1,000,000. A detailed program plan for the building was developed with rough sketches of what should be in the building. The vocational rehabilitation consultant[2] to the author and the staff of the Training Department were involved in every step of the planning. These functional plans were presented to the architect who designed the building according to the requested specifications.

The author left the FWSS in January, 1966, prior to the move into the new facility. The new Administrator[3] of the Ginsberg Rehabilitation Center (the name given the facility) completed the move and implemented the program in the new facility.

---

[1] Mr. H. T. Dean, Assistant Superintendent for Administration, provided much guidance and leadership in planning, designing, and implementing the construction of the total facility.

[2] Dr. M. C. Beyerl, Vice-President, Ball State University was then and continues to serve as the vocational rehabilitation consultant to FWSH & TC.

[3] Mr. Demos Gallender, who had been Chief of Vocational Activities, and in this capacity had been deeply involved in planning for the facility.

The basic plan of the program was to provide facilities for the intensive assessment and evaluation of the vocational potential of the mentally retarded and to provide the needed remedial adjustment and training services to allow them to reach their maximum potential. A multi-discipline team composed of a physician, a social worker, a clinical psychologist, vocational counselors, workshop supervisors, a speech and hearing therapist, and teachers would do the assessment and evaluation.

Included in this multi-discipline team was to be a counselor from the Indiana Division of Vocational Rehabilitation (DVR) who would serve as liaison counselor between the Center and the DVR counselors throughout the state. Referrals for evaluation and training of mentally retarded from anywhere in the state could be made from the local DVR counselor through the liaison counselor to the Center. (See Appendix A for description of client referral procedure.)

Figure 1 is a scheme of the Ginsberg Rehabilitation Center at Fort Wayne State Hospital & Training Center.

The complete facility consists of two general areas under one roof and covers 95,000 square feet. The training section consisting of 23,000 square feet includes, in addition to the general offices and offices for the vocational counselors, offices and diagnostic facilities for the various disciplines named, classrooms for teaching social competence, a home economics training apartment and domestic skills training area, an industrial arts area, and a simulated workshop.

The maintenance section covering 72,000 square feet includes the physical plant maintenance areas, food service areas, and the general warehouse for the Hospital. The building was designed this way so that part of the clients' assessment and training could be done in these areas under actual working conditions. On-the-job training was also to be provided on jobs throughout the Hospital.

Two dormitory units (one male, one female) of 56 beds each were built to house clients coming to the Center.

The Administrator* of Ginsberg Rehabilitation Unit submitted a grant proposal (Gallender, 1967) to the Indiana Department of Vocational Rehabilitation with the strong support of the new hospital superintendent, Dr. Ora Ackerman, and the appropriate state agencies, for funds to staff the facility adequately and implement the assessment, evaluation, and training program in depth. Under the purpose of the proposal he states:

---

* Mr. Demos Gallender assisted greatly in the preparation of this section of this chapter and the section in the next chapter dealing with vocational rehabilitation programming for the mentally retarded at the Ginsberg Rehabilitation Unit.

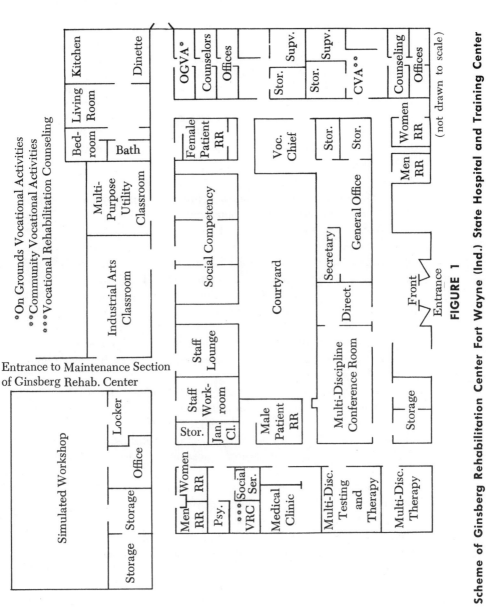

*On Grounds Vocational Activities
**Community Vocational Activities
***Vocational Rehabilitation Counseling

Entrance to Maintenance Section
of Ginsberg Rehab. Center

(not drawn to scale)

FIGURE 1

Scheme of Ginsberg Rehabilitation Center Fort Wayne (Ind.) State Hospital and Training Center

This plan includes processes of vocational diagnosis, therapeutic programming and training procedures, and understanding of the client's vocational, personal and employment needs. From these results, an orderly systematic and realistic rehabilitation program would be formulated for each client scheduled in the rehabilitation center.

These services would be open to all Indiana mentally retarded clients who could profit from the rehabilitation center's training program. Through programming and staffing, each client would be screened, evaluated, and placed according to his limitations. This proposal is designed to provide vocational programs to insure steady growth patterns and work performances. To assure success, it is important to develop plans for careful assessment and guidance of the client prior to his job placement. . . . Emphasis will be focused on intensive diagnosis, work evaluation, work adjustment, behavior modification and job placement.

The assessment and evaluation program developed by the Administrator and his staff included the following:

1. A five-day diagnostic period during which the client receives a medical evaluation, a psychological evaluation, a social evaluation, an educational and vocational background evaluation, and a social adjustment in environment evaluation. This diagnostic period culminates in a *planning review staffing* and a diagnostic report. This report provides ". . . a clear picture of the client's capabilities and limitations, his general medical condition and any change which may occur, special problems and consequent needs, the program of work evaluation training and such supportive services as the client may require." (Gallender, 1967)

2. A short term (2 to 4 weeks) work evaluation period during which the client's vocational, educational and leisure time potentials are assessed in the simulated workshop. No attempt is made to train or modify the client's habits, attitudes, and abilities. All efforts are diverted towards assessing those vocational habits, skills, abilities, and potentials possessed by the client.

Detailed job descriptions were first written of all jobs held by residents at the Training Center during 1960–61. In 1966 an in-depth analysis was again made of 157 jobs at the Training Center. Heavy emphasis was given to studying certain characteristics of these jobs. Each job has since been coded with Supplement II of the Dictionary of Occupational Titles (D.O.T.) and cross-coded. (See Appendix A for sample job description and D.O.T. coding.)

As the client is assessed and evaluated during this phase, his characteristics are carefully compared with those characteristics which previous studies have shown to be essential for success on specific jobs. Again, an intensive staffing follows the assessment period and detailed recommendations for the next phase are developed. The client's vocational potential has been carefully coded by all possible jobs in which he might achieve success. A detailed report is made at the completion of the Phase II Evaluation Period. (See Appendix A for sample report.) (For an interesting review of the literature on the use of job analysis for vocational evaluation of the MR, and a brief description of an experiment in the area at the Human Resources Center in Albertson, Long Island, see Blackman and Sipenstein [1968].)

3. The third phase, lasting from 3 to 6 months, is a work adjustment period during which he continues to undergo assessment and evaluation. An all-out effort is made under simulated work conditions to help the client improve his vocational performance. His training and evaluation take place in the classrooms as well as the simulated workshop of the Center. Constant evaluation with resulting changes in program attempt to help the client reach his potential. This stage of assessment and evaluation culminates in a detailed plan for future programming. (Space does not permit a more detailed description of this sophisticated vocational assessment and evaluation program. The vocational training and placement program will be discussed in the next chapter.)

As can be seen from the above, vocational assessment and evaluation for the mentally retarded requires a great deal more than the simple administration of a few tests. Considerable time must be spent under simulated work conditions utilizing both standardized test and non-standardized clinical evaluations to properly assess the vocational potential of the retarded.

Assessment of the Use of Leisure Time

Most of the community placements of residents of FWSH & TC that failed, did so because the resident could not adequately or properly use his leisure time. There are few leisure time activities that are open to the mentally retarded as transportation is usually required and often not available. However, a study at the FWSH & TC found that the residents needed considerable guidance to find those activities that were available. Their use of leisure time consisted primarily of watching television.

Ginsberg Rehabilitation Center has developed a questionnaire for assessing leisure time usage of the retarded. It also serves as a guide for helping the retarded select appropriate activities.

Development of a Plan for Action

Whenever assessment and evaluation of a retarded child are undertaken for any purpose, they are never complete until a staffing has been held by the multi-discipline team involved in the assessment, and a plan of action developed. From the original assessment team, a committee should be established to follow the progress of the child in the program. Periodic progress review staffings should be held to keep the child's program in line with the developing abilities.

The author recognizes that the type of assessment and evaluation he has suggested is "Man on Mars" for the majority of the mentally retarded — simply because we have not reached the point of caring enough for these "least ones" to provide services and programs for them. The purpose in presenting it is to provide a description of a model approach to a full assessment and evaluation program. Additionally, the trend is towards mandatory legislation requiring programs for all children. Perhaps the day is not too far in the future when these services will be available for all the retarded, and man will be walking on Mars.

3

Vocational Rehabilitation for the Mentally Retarded

There are those who argue that the term "habilitation" should be used when speaking of education and training for the mentally retarded. Their point is that "rehabilitation" indicates bringing a person back to a position or status he once enjoyed.

In recent years the term "rehabilitation" has come to include in its definition, the "development" and "preservation," as well as the "restoration" of the handicapped to the fullest physical, mental, social, and economic usefulness of which they are capable. Thus, we can define vocational rehabilitation for the mentally retarded as the process of developing, preserving, and/or restoring the retarded to their fullest physical, mental, social, and vocational potential.

This definition reveals that rehabilitation of the handicapped has come to be based on the concept of the dignity of every human being, however handicapped. The actual rehabilitation of the individual can come about only as he chooses, and thus, is largely a product of his own making. However, the community in which he resides must provide for him (as it does for his "normal" counterpart) the professional help and facilities he needs to achieve a productive life in society.

Value of Work to This Individual

The importance of work to the individual cannot be over-emphasized. The importance and worthwhileness of being "employed at a useful work" are drilled into him from his earliest years whether he is from the wealthiest or the poorest family in the nation.

We live in a "work-oriented" society. The individual who has a responsible vocation is highly regarded, while the individual who does no work tends to be held in low regard. Productivity by every individual is the ultimate goal, whether for economic reasons (the extremely high cost of maintaining life in an individual makes this goal important) or because of our enlightened belief in the importance of every human being (though we are just coming to this point of view in its fullest sense for the mentally retarded). Much of our personality is structured around the concept of work. We are taught that we must work to earn pleasures and to gain the approval of others — our parents, our friends, and our society. It has been pointed out that one of the prime motives for our desiring to work is an unconscious desire "to please mother"; however, we also find pleasure in work because it supplies many of our needs at the conscious level.

Mentally Retarded Involved in the Rehabilitation Process

The mentally retarded can be divided into four group classifications from a vocational rehabilitation point of view. First, there are those who can become totally self-sustaining in the community. Many of the retarded in this classification will never be labelled mentally retarded and will receive little, if any, special training. They will struggle through the regular school program, barely passing in most cases, and probably graduating from high school. They will enter the world of work, perhaps go into service, many have children, and in general lead a useful, relatively happy life.

The second group are those who can eventually become self-sustaining to some degree in the community. This group will require special education and vocational training. Most of them will require a sheltered living situation throughout their lives. Early vocational guidance will help them find productive work of which they are capable, and periodic guidance as emergencies on the job or crises in the home arise, will keep them functioning relatively smoothly in society. Many of this group will marry, usually a person stronger than themselves who can provide the support and direction they need. Many of this group are easy marks for confidence men and are easily swayed into breaking the law by unscrupulous individuals offering friendships in return. Vocational rehabilitation, including lifetime counseling, is extremely important to members of this group if they are to have relatively happy, useful lives.

The third group are those who because of their degree of retardation and impaired level of adaptive behavior, will require a totally sheltered living and working situation throughout their lives. Proper placement in the community, terminal, sheltered workshop can help them live relatively happy and productive lives.

The fourth group are those whose severe degree of retardation and level of adaptive behavior, perhaps complicated further by a severe physical handicap, will require total care, eventually in an institution. Many of the retarded in this group can be trained to do useful work in the home or institution, thus, helping to reduce the economic cost of their support.

The author recalls the case of such a resident of a hospital where he was once employed, who was fondly known to the staff as "Dutch." Dutch never scored above 32 on the several IQ tests he had taken, but he did an excellent job playing catcher on the patients' baseball team. He also drove a team of horses that pulled the laundry wagon. His job was to pick up the dirty linen from the cottages, scattered over a 1,200 acre area, in the morning and get them to the laundry by noon. In the afternoon he reversed the procedure, taking the clean linen to the cottages. Seldom did he make a mistake in his work.

The author also recalls four residents of Fort Wayne State Hospital and Training Center who had IQ scores below 32 who were able to perform satisfactorily on jobs in the community. Some of them took city busses to and from work.

These examples illustrate that some severely retarded individuals contribute to society and lead useful lives. In some cases we are overly pessimistic regarding their capabilities.

Objectives of Vocational Rehabilitation of the Mentally Retarded

The goals and objectives offered below are a challenge and not a statement of what currently exists. Only a very few existing programs meet these objectives, and they operate for entirely too few of the mentally retarded.

1. To provide a program to meet the vocational needs of every phase of the mentally retarded individual's life.

2. To provide vocational education in the classroom, in the simulated workshop, in the school-work study program, or in a specialized vocational educational setting.

    a. To develop desirable job attitudes and habits.

    b. To teach job skills.

    c. To provide a systematic, work placement program that takes into consideration the mentally retarded student's interests, aptitudes, and the opportunities available in the local community.

3. To provide vocational counseling to the mentally retarded with pre-vocational or vocational problems through individual or group counseling and utilizing all of the multi-disciplined professional resources available.

4. To provide the nation with an additional supply of trained workers from a group usually ignored. The retarded frequently perform best in jobs their "normal" counterparts have little interest in.

5. To locate and develop potential employer trainers who will become part of the rehabilitation team in training and employing the mentally retarded.

6. To determine through research, the most effective vocational rehabilitation methods, and programs for the mentally retarded.

7. To improve through massive public education, the opportunities open to the mentally retarded for a full, happy life.

Vocational Rehabilitation for the Mentally Retarded

Vocational rehabilitation programs have been developing on several levels. The majority of these are excellent; however, all of them are faced with the problems of insufficient trained staff and inadequate budgets. Many have excellent facilities, though the majority of the programs are struggling in inadequate facilities to provide services.

These programs will be discussed by their commitment — local, state, or national. No attempt will be made to include all programs since space limitations will not permit.

Local Vocational Rehabilitation Programs for the Mentally Retarded

Local programs of vocational rehabilitation for the mentally retarded fall into two general classes — (1) public school, school-work study programs and (2) community centers for the mentally retarded.

Work Study Programs in Public Schools

Younie (1966) edited an excellent publication entitled "Guidelines for Establishing School-Work Study Programs for Educable Mentally Retarded Youth." This monograph was published by the Special Education Service, State Department of Education, Richmond, Virginia, and is available through that office. It is helpful reading for the counselor who is in a school system with a work study program or is interested in beginning such a program. The following material is basically extracted from this publication.

Work study programs for the retarded in the public schools are not new, as they have been discussed in the literature for the past 30 years. It was not until the Vocational Education Act of 1963 was passed giving emphasis to these programs that their development began to be widespread. Yet, experience has shown that their best chance for success still exists in those schools having work study programs in general education.

Younie (1966) states the organizational guidelines for the school-work program as follows:

1. Is a bridge between school and work.
2. Must be preceded by good preparatory programs.
3. Must include careful screening techniques.
4. Must be step by step.
5. Must set and limit the teacher's role.
6. Cannot exist in isolation.
7. Includes training in general vocational tasks.
8. Depends on community support.
9. Considers the parents to be vital.
10. Is not the sole answer to the problem of vocational rehabilitation.
11. Includes a systematic transfer program with the Department of Vocational Rehabilitation.
12. Includes vocational evaluation.
13. Considers follow-up to be essential.

Work study programs attempt to interrelate the academic world and the vocational world so that the retarded child can make a smooth transition from one to the other. These programs are a part of the secondary school, special education program. However, it must be pointed out that success in the work study program depends upon its being an integrated part of the total special education program. Planning and training throughout the student's school years must direct him towards future success in the job.

In the instructional phase of the program emphasis is placed upon the kinds of jobs available to the retarded locally, how to apply for one's Social Security card, how to apply for a job, and how to be successful on the job — good grooming, punctuality, loyalty, and steady work.

When the student has reached legal age, he is referred to the Division of Vocational Rehabilitation (DVR) and placed in part-time work. After placement, the instructional program for the individual student centers around his job so that the learning on the job is reinforced in the classroom and vice versa.

There is no one pattern for work study programs for the mentally retarded even within a state. This has allowed a great deal of experimentation and has resulted in programs ranging from mediocre to excellent. Again, availability of trained staff and funds, along with public acceptance of the program, make the basic difference.

Younie (1966) offers the following general principles for the school-work study program:

1. The public school has a basic responsibility for providing programs for all children during the school years as defined by local law or regulation. These programs shall be designed and conducted so as to meet best the needs of the individuals assigned to them.
2. The educable mentally retarded shall have a special program, but this program will not result in their being isolated from the society to which they must adjust after leaving school.
3. As with children of higher intelligence, the goal of economic self-sufficiency is recognized as being a vital objective for the educable mentally retarded. On the basis of information presently available, it is assumed that this goal may be reached most efficiently and effectively through a well-structured, vocationally-oriented program which is designed as a school-work study program or some similar term.
4. While the goal of economic self-sufficiency is considered primary to the school-work study program, it is not the only objective which is sought and should not overshadow other benefits which the school can provide.
5. The school-work study program cannot exist in isolation but must be a part of a total organizational plan which actively involves teachers at all developmental levels. This plan will consider the school-work experience program as its final instructional phase.
6. The teacher will function as a member of a total school team organized to give assistance to the educable mentally retarded child. The team will operate on the premise that while the teacher has specific responsibility for the child in the school-work study program, the entire school has general responsibilities which it must fulfill.
7. While the time in the child's life alloted to his education must not be wasted, neither must it be compressed so that there is not enough space for the testing, the teaching, and the maturation that must take place. The child must have time to fail and to try again.
8. Because of the mental and social handicaps which characterize the retarded, the school is responsible for insuring that its retarded graduates receive adequate post-school services. This responsibility may be realized through the techniques of referral and the training of students in the use of community resources. The techniques imply

close liaison between the school and local rehabilitation agencies of various types.

For the counselor desiring more information in school-work study programs, in addition to the monograph listed above, see Kolstoe and Frey (1965). Most of the states have developed guidelines for their own programs; for example, Woods (1968) has developed a very good guide for work study programs in Indiana. These also make excellent sources for further study.

Community Centers for the Mentally Retarded

The current trend is towards the establishment of community centers for the mentally retarded that provide programs for those retarded children who do not qualify for public school special education programs, because of age or severe handicaps that cannot be provided for in the public school program. They usually have a sheltered workshop program that provides training and employment in a competitive work setting.

The U.S. Department of Labor, which regulates the workshops, defines the workshop as a "charitable organization or institution conducted, not for profit, but for the purpose of carrying out a recognized program of rehabilitation for handicapped workers and/or providing such individuals with remunerative employment or other occupational rehabilitating activity of an educational or therapeutic nature." Thus, the workshop can be either terminal or transitional in nature. By terminal, we mean the client may be employed therein for the balance of his vocational life. Transitional, on the other hand, refers to a training program in a sheltered setting that leads to employment in business or industry.

A cooperative program may be worked out between the public school special education program and the community center for the retarded, to provide vocational training for those students who cannot qualify for the school-work study program.

Some of the community centers for the mentally retarded contain intermediate workshops that provide initial training and education leading to placement in the sheltered workshops. These intermediate workshops are for persons who cannot perform with adequate speed, produce quality work, or demonstrate appropriate behavior required for placement in the regular sheltered workshop program. These intermediate workshops may be the entry program for the student from the public school program if there is no secondary special education program.

The community centers for the mentally retarded are usually funded from several sources. These include local tax agencies, state and federal tax funds, and funds from local United Community service agencies. Minimal tuition is often charged, but no child is denied services because of inability to pay.

An example of a community center for the mentally retarded is the Wabash Center for the Mentally Retarded, Inc., in Lafayette, Indiana. A brief description of this facility and its program follows to illustrate the much welcomed strengthening of programming such a center provides for the retarded in any community.

This is a private organization financed by the United Community Services, county, tax level, state grants, tuition, and gifts. The stated general purpose and function: "to provide comprehensive services for the mentally retarded including diagnosis, treatment, training, education, day custodial services, sheltered workshops and family counseling." Those served include mental retardates ranging from pre-school ages through adult years. The Center is under the direction of a Board of Directors who establish policy and guide the program through the Director of the Center.[1]

A $561,500 facility that includes classrooms, home economics apartment, general offices, therapy and treatment rooms, large multi-purpose room, as well as a separate building for the sheltered workshop, was completed in 1968.

Figure 2 is a scheme of the Educational Unit of Wabash Center for the Mentally Retarded. Figure 3 is a scheme of the Sheltered Workshop. There are 12,000 square feet in the education unit and 5,000 square feet in the sheltered workshop.

Tilton (1967), in a locally distributed, unpublished brochure, stated the following about the role of the Center:

> Community based programs for the mentally retarded have received increasing emphasis and support in recent years as evidence mounts indicating the majority of these handicapped individuals can be more effectively cared for within their communities than in the large state institutions.

> With the care and training of the retardate shared by the family and the community center, opportunities for the retarded individual to achieve his particular potential level of adjustment, self-sufficiency and productivity are increased, and the degree and period of dependency significantly reduced.

---

[1] James R. Tilton, Executive Director of the Center since 1965. He was the chief implementor in the raising of funds for the construction of the buildings and the development of the program.

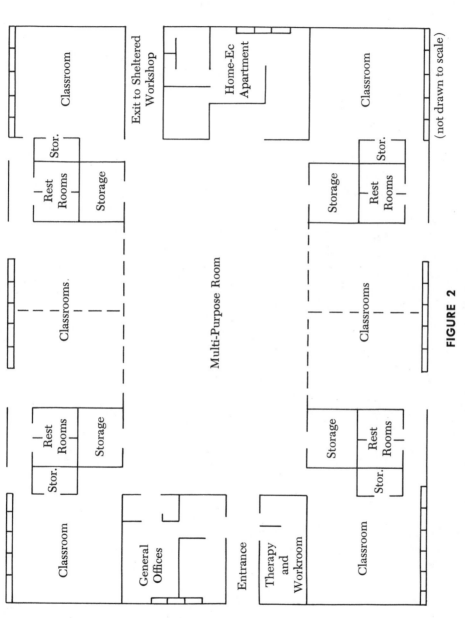

FIGURE 2

Scheme of the Educational Unit of the Wabash Center for the Mentally Retarded

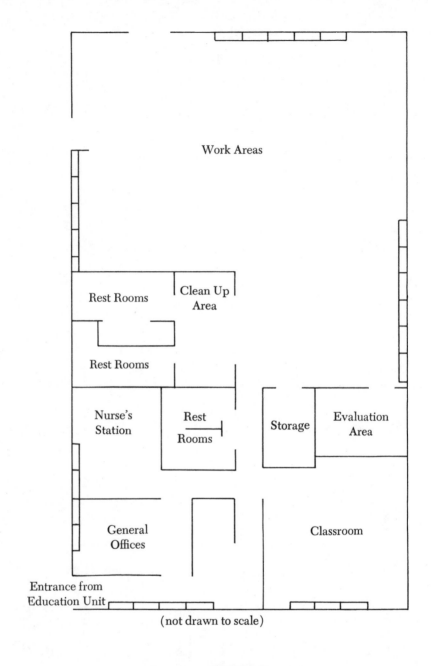

Work Areas

Rest Rooms

Clean Up Area

Rest Rooms

Nurse's Station

Rest Rooms

Storage

Evaluation Area

General Offices

Classroom

Entrance from Education Unit

(not drawn to scale)

FIGURE 3

**Scheme of the Sheltered Workshop of the Wabash
Center for the Mentally Retarded**

In fulfilling its role as a comprehensive community center for the retarded, Wabash Center provides services to those individuals whose age, level of retardation, multiplicity of handicaps or specific handicaps prevent their participating in public school classes for the retarded, but whose requirements for either temporary or long-term services do not necessitate institutionalization in a residential setting.

Table 4 shows the Relationships of Wabash Center to other agencies with respect to individuals served.

A close cooperative relationship is maintained by the Center with all other community agencies which provide service to the mentally retarded. Every effort is made to develop cooperative planning and programming that avoids unnecessary duplication of services and results in all needed services being provided. Table 5 shows the inter-relationships the Center maintains with other community services.

An elaborate program is provided for approximately 160 mentally retarded persons. In addition, three classes of trainable retardates from the public schools are housed in the Center.

Table 6 shows the types of services provided by Wabash Center.

Further information regarding the developing of the facilities and the program may be obtained by writing to the Executive Director, Wabash Center for the Mentally Retarded, 2000 Greenbush Street, Lafayette, Indiana 47904.

Where an adequate community center for the vocational rehabilitation of the mentally retarded exists, arrangements should be made for the public schools to use these facilities, paying tuition costs rather than duplicating the services. Changes in state laws are sometimes necessary before this can be done.

State Vocational Rehabilitation Training Programs for the Mentally Retarded

Certain states have established vocational assessment, evaluation, and training centers for the mentally retarded who cannot receive these services in their local community. As discussed in Chapter II, the Ginsberg Rehabilitation Center at Fort Wayne State Hospital and Training Center is such a center. The assessment and evaluation phase of the program was discussed in Chapter 2; however, since an excellent vocational training program that serves the mentally retarded throughout Indiana, has been developed there, we shall examine the training program briefly.

For each client completing the assessment and evaluation program, a staffing is held to consider carefully a proposed training program. Several questions are raised: (1) Are there facilities and staff available

TABLE 4

Relationship of Wabash Center to Other Agencies with Respect to Individuals Served*

Local Public Schools	Wabash Center	Fort Wayne State School
School age educable and trainable retardates	Pre-school ages	The profoundly retarded
(It is not mandatory in Indiana for school districts to provide classes for these children. Local schools are not yet serving all the children in these classifications.)	Post-school ages	Individuals whose physical conditions require extensive medical or nursing care.
[Becomes mandatory in 1973]	The severely retarded and/or multiply handicapped, including those of school age. Includes interim care for individuals on waiting lists for admission to state residential facilities.	Individuals whose families, because of death, serious illness and other factors, cannot provide for their needs in the community.
		Those individuals presenting serious social problems in the community.

* Developed by James R. Tilton, Executive Director, Wabash Center for the Mentally Retarded, 1967. Used with permission.

TABLE 5

Wabash Center for the Mentally Retarded

INTER-RELATIONSHIPS WITH COMMUNITY AGENCIES

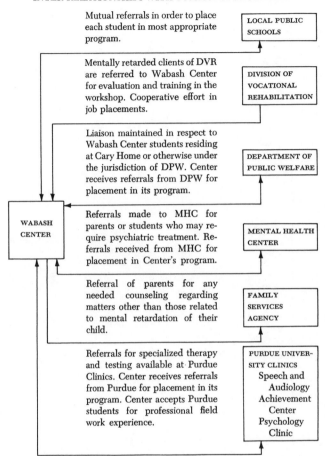

Mutual referrals in order to place each student in most appropriate program.	LOCAL PUBLIC SCHOOLS
Mentally retarded clients of DVR are referred to Wabash Center for evaluation and training in the workshop. Cooperative effort in job placements.	DIVISION OF VOCATIONAL REHABILITATION
Liaison maintained in respect to Wabash Center students residing at Cary Home or otherwise under the jurisdiction of DPW. Center receives referrals from DPW for placement in its program.	DEPARTMENT OF PUBLIC WELFARE
WABASH CENTER — Referrals made to MHC for parents or students who may require psychiatric treatment. Referrals received from MHC for placement in Center's program.	MENTAL HEALTH CENTER
Referral of parents for any needed counseling regarding matters other than those related to mental retardation of their child.	FAMILY SERVICES AGENCY
Referrals for specialized therapy and testing available at Purdue Clinics. Center receives referrals from Purdue for placement in its program. Center accepts Purdue students for professional field work experience.	PURDUE UNIVERSITY CLINICS Speech and Audiology Achievement Center Psychology Clinic

Developed by James R. Tilton, Executive Director, Wabash Center for the Mentally Retarded, Inc., 1967. Used with Permission.

in his home community to provide the needed training? (2) Is there some other facility available that can provide this training? (3) If not, would he benefit from the short term training offered at the Training Center?

If the decision is that the client can benefit from the short term training program and that this is the best program open to him, he enters the work adjustment phase of the program. Gallender (1967) states:

TABLE 6

Types of Services Provided by Wabash Center*

Training Activities	Education	Sheltered Workshops
Self-care activities	Activities for post school age students designed to develop functional use of academic skills in work situations and activities of daily living.	Performance of contracted work for business and industries and production of goods for sale with wages earned on the basis of individual productivity.
Auditory, visual and tactile discrimination		
Auditory and visual memory training		
Gross motor activities		
Visual Motor activities	Includes work in units of measurements, money management, consumer purchasing, health and safety practices, use of newspapers, directories and maps, employment forms and procedures.	Work activity programs to develop constructive work habits and basic work skills.
Language development		
Social development		
Prevocational training		
Home arts training		
	Special education activities for school age retardates whose multiple handicaps prevent attendance in public school classes for retarded.	Placement in the workshop programs may be transitional, leading to employment in the community, or may require extended sheltered employment.

Evaluation	Counseling	Custodial Day Care
Psychological testing including those concerned with intellectual, perceptual, language, social education and vocational development or performance.	Individual and group parent counseling in relation to home management and training of the student and in developing short term and long range planning for the student.	Activity program for the severely retarded including provision for basic personal care where needed.
Collection and evaluation of medical data obtained from family physicians, hospitals, clinics, etc.	Individual and group counseling of adolescent and adult students in relation to adjustment within Center's program and in preparation and follow-up to placement in jobs or in other community activities.	Activities include more basic forms of training activities particularly in area of basic self-care training.
Collection of developmental history of student and information regarding adjustment within the family, previously attended schools in the community and within Center's program.		Some home bound training coupled with parent counseling needs to be provided for severely retarded individuals whose condition prevents transportation to the Center.

* Prepared by James R. Tilton, Executive Director, Wabash Center for the Mentally Retarded, 1967. Used with permission.

The third phase of the program is a three to six month period which attempts to reshape, modify or reverse the mal-or-non-adjustive behaviors that were identified in the diagnostic and work evaluation phases. The work adjustment processes are focused on molding or changing vocational knowledge, attitudes and philosophies of work. It is a period designed to meet the vocational needs of the client through work adjustment to himself, his peer group, and the immediate physical setting. The intensified program will attempt to substitute the levels of vocational deficiency with areas of competency readiness and positive growth.

The training takes place in the simulated workshop, the social competence classrooms, the industrial arts classrooms, the home economics apartment and domestic science training areas, and in the academic classroom. Psychotherapy, speech therapy, medical treatment, and/or vocational counseling are provided as needed.

Upon the successful completion of the work adjustment phase, the client moves to on-the-job training. Here he will be closely supervised, but given every opportunity for vocational growth. This training takes place in carefully selected jobs that offer the greatest chance for success. Vocational industrial therapists work closely with the client helping him to adjust to and learn the job assigned.

The on-the-job training terminates when the client has demonstrated he has employable skills with desirable work habits and attitudes. At this time, he is returned to his home community or another community offering employment through the Division of Vocational Rehabilitation's liaison counselor. The vocational rehabilitation counselor in the community is apprised of the results of the assessment, evaluation, and vocational training. He is also given a detailed report of the client's strengths and weaknesses and a list of entry jobs coded to the D.O.T. for which he is qualified. (See Appendix A–IV for sample terminal report on client. Counselor also gets a copy of Work Evaluation Report, Appendix A–III.)

Unfortunately, the numbers of referrals that can be accepted at one time is 112 because of limited residence hall space; however, approximately 1,000 of the permanent residents of the Training Center are also benefiting from this program.

National Vocational Rehabilitation Programs for the Mentally Retarded

The national programs for vocational rehabilitation training for the mentally retarded include two major federal programs — the Armed

Forces Recruitment and Training Program for the Mentally Retarded and the Civil Service Employment Programs for the Mentally Retarded — and such major private programs as the Jewish Vocational Service of Milwaukee, Wisconsin, among others. Since the guidance counselor is likely to be called upon to counsel a student seeking admission to the Armed Forces Training Program or employment in the Civil Service Employment Program, these shall be discussed briefly.

Civil Service Employment Programs for the Mentally Retarded

In January 1964, the United States Civil Service Commission (C.S.C.) began a new program for the employment of the mentally retarded who were occupationally qualified for routine jobs in the Federal Service.

President John F. Kennedy initiated this government-wide program for employing the mentally retarded in 1963. In announcing the program, he said, "It is just as important to integrate the mentally retarded within our modern society and make full use of their abilities as it is to make a special effort to do this for the physically handicapped. The grim struggle for survival does not allow us the luxury of wasting our human resources."

The intention of this program was ". . . to show the nation what can be done to make fuller use of the abilities of such persons, with mutual benefit to them, their employers, and the public." Their announced goal: "Good placements, placements that will be long-range success and will prove, for all to see, that properly trained and properly placed retarded persons do make good employees," (C.S.C., 1964). The Federal agencies agreeing to participate in this program enter into a written agreement with the C.S.C. This agreement includes the following:

A statement of the positions, title grades, and tasks to be assigned appointees (or a statement that these will be worked out with a state vocational rehabilitation agency.)

An agreement that each person appointed will be certified by the state vocational rehabilitation agency as socially competent, able to perform the duties, and physically qualified to do so without hazard to himself or others.

A commitment to use the state vocational rehabilitation agency for post-placement counseling of appointees and for advising and training supervisors of the retarded.

An agreement not to terminate employment without prior notice to the retardate's vocational rehabilitation counselor.

An agreement to submit certain information and reports. (C.S.C., 1966)

The retarded do not have to take civil service examinations under the terms of this agreement. They apply to their local state office of vocational rehabilitation where they will undergo extensive assessment and evaluation prior to being employed.

The District of Columbia's Department of Vocational Rehabilitation recently concluded a 3-year study of 2800 of the mentally retarded employees of the Federal Government. They found the retarded successfully employed in over 100 job classifications including such positions as typists, laboratory technicians, messengers, laundry workers, and clerks. None of the jobs had had to be modified for the mentally retarded. Twenty-two percent had been promoted and reassigned to more difficult jobs after training. Seven percent had received "sustained superior performance" and "outstanding performance" awards.

The report demonstrated that when the mentally retarded are properly placed on jobs that utilize their abilities to take directions, follow through, and work at a steady pace, they can become productive and valued employees.

Copies of this report, which would be valuable to the guidance counselor, are available from the District of Columbia, Vocational Rehabilitation, 1331 "H" Street, N. W., Washington, D.C. 20005. The report is entitled *The National Follow-up Study of Mental Retardates Employed by the Federal Government.*

Armed Forces Recruitment and Training Program
for the Mentally Retarded

As a result of President Kennedy's call for government-wide employment of the mentally retarded, his Secretary of Defense, Robert S. McNamara, developed a program for the retarded in the Armed Forces. This project became known as McNamara's Project 100,000 as he called for the induction of 100,000 men into the Armed Forces who would normally have been rejected.

The program met with a great deal of resistance from the various branches of the service that feared this would weaken the military might of the country. Secretary McNamara prevailed, pointing out that there were many jobs in the Armed Forces that could be done adequately by the mentally retarded. He also pointed out that every retarded person the Armed Forces was able to train and use added to the economic strength of the country, in addition to helping to build the man.

The program has been extremely successful: over 200,000 men have been trained in this program and "salvaged for mankind." Although there is still some resistance to the program, the success of the majority of the recruits has insured the continuation of the program.

Since programs like this tend to change or be dropped over a period of time, the author suggests the counselor check with the local recruiters for the various branches of the Armed Forces for correct information when needed.

Summary

Several principles which must be kept in mind regarding the vocational rehabilitation of the mentally retarded are as follows:

1. It must be begun at a very early age. Parents should begin the teaching of proper habits and attitudes towards work at a pre-school age. Programs for the kindergarten and elementary school age retarded child should continue this emphasis. Realistic concepts of the kinds of work to which the retarded can aspire should be taught in social science units, and should be an integral part of the total curriculum.

2. It is an individual process. As has been reiterated in several ways throughout this monograph, while the mentally retarded share certain characteristics, they must be treated on an individual basis both for assessment and evaluation and for their vocational placement and rehabilitation.

3. A multi-disciplined team is required to do the assessment and evaluation, program planning, training, placement, and follow-up.

4. There are not nearly enough trained specialists, specialized facilities, nor adequate programs to reach even one-half of the mentally retarded.

5. A tremendous increase in budgets at the local, state, and federal level is essential not only for the service to the retarded, but also for training the specialist, building the facilities, and providing the program.

For example, Indiana needs 5,000 additional teachers of the mentally retarded by 1973 to implement the mandatory laws passed by the 1969 Indiana General Assembly. All of the college and university special education teacher training programs in Indiana graduated less than 300 qualified teachers in 1968. Special funds must be appropriated to the colleges and universities for program development in special education departments, if these needs are going to be met.

6. A massive public education program is needed to make the public aware of the plight of most of the mentally retarded. The President's Panel on Mental Retardation is doing a good job on the national scene; however, many more people must get involved at both the state and local levels. More employers must become members of the rehabilitation team and accorded professional recognition for their contribution to the rehabilitation of the mentally retarded.

4

Vocational Counseling, Planning, and Placement of the Mentally Retarded

As has been continuously stressed throughout this monograph, vocational rehabilitation of the mentally retarded is a life-long job. It must begin with the very young child in the development of proper attitudes, habits and self-concept (of his potential worth as a contributing member of society.) A multi-disciplinary team is required to assess, evaluate and plan the training programs and then to follow up the effectiveness of the program. The next phase in the vocational rehabilitation process is the counseling, planning and placement of the retarded student. Though part of this counseling process and the planning process has been in progress all along, we shall examine these processes as though they were separate entities. Actually they are an integral part of the total program with a smooth transition from one phase to the other.

Role of the School Counselor in Planning for the Vocational Rehabilitation of the Mentally Retarded

The insufficient number of counselors in elementary schools adds to the problems of the mentally retarded. The counselor in the elementary school is the logical member of the multi-discipline team to remind the program planning committee for the retarded that one of their chief long range goals is to help the retarded become employable. He should help with curriculum planning in order to insure that there is steady progression in the program towards this goal. He should serve as the coordinator between the vocational aspects of the elementary program and the eventual work of the guidance counselor in the high school-work study program for the retarded.

Counselors in the secondary school should become more deeply involved in the special education programs at the junior high as well as the high school programs. As the retarded student moves from the elementary program to the junior high school program, the secondary school counselor should become part of the multi-disciplinary team continuing to plan and evaluate his on-going program. The counselor should plan with the teacher and share some class hours in which he will talk with the students about their vocational aspirations and opportunities. He should help the teacher plan units of study stressing appropriate vocational areas. He should, of course, conduct individual and group counseling sessions with the retarded students when they become concerned about their vocational futures.

As the retarded student moves into the secondary program, the counselor becomes an increasingly important member of the multi-disciplined planning committee. The local Division of Vocational Rehabilitation (DVR) counselor should also become a member of the planning committee at this point in order that he can begin planning for the eventual placement of the student in a job.

The counselor, the director of special education, and the DVR counselor, should hold frequent conferences to coordinate their efforts — the DVR counselor should bring his knowledge of the local community's business, industrial, and service needs; the director of special education, and the school counselor should bring their understanding of the developing curriculum and program the mentally retarded students are receiving and the characteristics of the students. A study of the three areas will do much to ascertain the readiness of the mentally retarded students for meeting the vocational needs of the community. From these meetings will come a better understanding of the part that the special education curriculum is playing in the total rehabilitation of the retarded student.

Too frequently, the curriculum for the retarded is not developmentally articulated. Each classroom, each division, tends to be a separate entity whose curriculum and program are not understood in relation to the other parts by the professionals; therefore, how can they possibly be understood by the child?

From the meetings of the DVR counselor, the school counselor, and the director of special education should come some efforts to coordinate the total special education curriculum so that it progresses towards the ultimate goal for the retarded child; i.e., education and training that allow the retarded student to be a productive member of his society, to be happy and secure in a job he can perform adequately, to have a life that is satisfying, and to have the proper skills to use his leisure time. These things cannot be counted on to just happen for the mentally retarded. They must be carefully planned from his infancy on.

Where a strong, well-organized special education program exists with adequately trained teachers, supervisors, and administrators, the school counselor will not need to get as deeply involved in curriculum planning. In this happy situation he will serve as a coordinator between the special education program, the school-work study program, and the DVR placement program. However, there is still the need for constant meetings between the three parties for program coordination.

In the school system with a poorly organized special education program, the secondary school counselor must become deeply involved in coordinating curriculum development, particularly in the vocational area, if the students are to be ready for placement when they come to him. If there is an elementary school counselor in the district, the secondary school counselor should work with him in helping the elementary special education teacher keep the needed vocational training in the curriculum pertinent. Materials can be supplied, appropriate workers from the community can be consulted, field trip planning help can be given, and other assistance afforded to help strengthen the vocational aspects of the curriculum. The school counselor must work and plan with many other professionals as well as with the retarded child over the entire school life of the student if vocational counseling, planning, and placement are to be effectively carried out.

Role of the School Counselor in Vocational Counseling for the Mentally Retarded

Faust (1968) presents an interesting concept in counseling at the elementary school level that reverses the traditional role of counselors in the secondary school. He would have the elementary school counselor give group counseling priority over individual counseling, and consultative work with teachers priority over work with individual students. There is much to commend this procedure — especially in the work the elementary school counselor does with the mentally retarded and the special education teacher. Faust also stresses the consultation role of the elementary school counselor with teachers, for example,

". . . consultation as in-service training regarding mental apparatus operations, how children modify behavior, what makes them do what they do . . ." He stresses that the hierarchy of priorities should again be headed by consultation with groups of teachers rather than with the individual teacher.

Both of these roles (and in the order of presentation) are vitally important to the special education teacher and the mentally retarded child. The elementary school counselor can play an essential role in helping the special education teacher become accepted as part of the total professional teaching staff of the school. Perhaps more than any other teacher, the special education teacher needs someone to turn to for counseling and consultation on education problems. Too often, there will be only one special education teacher in a school; in this situation the teacher may feel that she must bear all her problems alone or hold them in abeyance until the supervisor comes by. Many of her problems are shared with other general education teachers. Conducting a counseling group of teachers with problems can help all of the teachers understand better the special education teacher's problems and their own.

The school counselor must also consult with the special education teachers on vocational planning and emphasis in the curriculum, as previously mentioned, if there is to be a continuous developmental curriculum in this area. He must help the teacher understand the kinds of vocational information that should be included at a particular level. In order to do this adequately, he must consult frequently with the secondary school counselor who has pertinent vocational information about the community available through his work with the school-work study program and/or with the DVR counselor.

The elementary school counselor must do some group vocational counseling with the retarded student as a regular contribution to the special education curriculum. Most of this work can be done through vocational units by the teachers; however, the school counselor can greatly reinforce the teacher's work with occasional group counseling sessions during these units.

While there are only rare occasions when the elementary school counselor will have to do vocational counseling with individual retarded students, he may have to do individual counseling regarding personal problems these students face. Many of the students in the elementary special education program will be older than their peers in the general education program and will face problems of adolescence that are not usually faced until junior high school.

Unfortunately, the majority of existing special education programs have not been established as a normal progression system. In many districts there are only two divisions — a primary and a secondary; in many districts there is only a primary program, terminating at age sixteen, but worst of all, the majority of the school districts in the United States still provide programs for only one out of five mentally retarded, with many districts having no program at all.

Where there are no special education programs, the school counselor is constantly called upon to do crisis counseling with retarded children who are forced to sit in regular classes from which they cannot possibly benefit. While some of these students act up and are sent to the principal for disciplinary action, many more withdraw, and all require the help of the school counselor or other specialized personnel such as the school psychologist.

At the secondary level, the school counselor continues to work with and through the special education teacher. At this level, the counselor is interested in getting more vocational units in the curriculum and in providing the teacher with relevant occupational data he has obtained from the DVR counselor or his own surveys of the local community. Group, as well as individual, vocational counseling, has greater emphasis. Prior to the retarded student's entry into the school-work study program the counselor spends more time coordinating vocational testing programs and helping the retarded student use the results of these tests at his level of understanding.

In a small school district, when the mentally retarded enter the school-work study program, the counselor may be called upon to work with the employer-trainers in their roles and to help resolve their relationship problems with students. This is especially true if the district employs no one else in this specialized capacity.

Since parents of retarded children are a vital link in the total rehabilitation of the child, parental counseling is an essential though time-consuming task. For the parents of a mentally retarded child, movement of the child from the sheltered atmosphere of the school into an employment setting is often an anxiety provoking experience which calls for assistance from the school counselor. This role can be shared with the special education personnel — teachers, supervisory and administrative staff; however, where there are few trained special educators (as in the majority of the school districts) the school counselor will be called on to work with the parents. Whether he chooses to work with them directly in counseling or chooses a consultation role will depend upon his orientation and the specific problem faced.

The elementary school counselor is frequently faced with counseling parents who, for the first time, have come to realize that their child is retarded. Jordan (1966) gives ten commandments that serve as excellent guidelines. These guidelines hold true in any counseling situa-

tion with parents, but especially so with parents of the mentally retarded:

1. Be honest in your appraisal of the situation and explain it without unnecessary delay.
2. Deal with both parents, since they are a natural unit.
3. Be precise, but do not be unnecessarily technical in your explanation.
4. Point out who must ultimately be responsible.
5. Help the parents grasp the issues.
6. Keep in mind the referral agencies that can be of assistance.
7. Avoid precipitating ego defensive reaction in the parents.
8. Do not expect too much too soon from the parents.
9. Allow parents their quota of concern and uncertainty.
10. Try to crystallize positive attitudes at the outset by using good
    counseling techniques.

Campanelle (1965) points out that both the parents and the counselor must accept the fact that the mentally retarded child can ". . .
never measure up to the standards of, nor even compete equally with, a
normal one." They also must accept the fact that nothing the parents
could have done would have altered the situation—that mental retardation is not particular to any economic or social strata of society or
of any racial group and exists in all countries. Facing the facts helps
to alleviate feelings of guilt on the part of the parents.

(For more information on the counseling of parents of the mentally
retarded see the sources listed.)

Role of the Counselor in the Vocational Placement of the Mentally Retarded

If there is a school-work study program for the mentally retarded
in the school district, the school counselor would have begun the process of placement long before the student arrives at the point of entering the program (as has been discussed previously). Assuming that
there is a school-work study program, and this is a gross assumption at
our present state of development, the school counselor will be working
closely with the DVR counselor to be familiar with the employment
needs of the local community. Together they will have surveyed the
local business, industrial, and service potentials for placement and
training of the retarded.

The DVR counselor enters the picture early, not to abrogate the function of the school counselor in the placement phase of the school-work
study program, but in order to be thoroughly acquainted with the students who will become his responsibilities after completion of the

school program. While the school work-study program usually terminates the school program for the retarded child, it must be remembered that it serves to bridge the gap between the educational and the vocational worlds.

Not all mentally retarded students in the special education program can meet the requirements of the school-work study program. As was mentioned earlier, if there is a community center for the retarded with a sheltered workshop program, the school system should work out arrangements for those students who do not qualify for school-work study to enter this program or establish another program in order to satisfactorily meet their neds.

It is necessary to establish screening procedures to determine eligibility for placement in the programs available, whether the school-work study program, the sheltered work-shop, or the state or private assessment, evaluation and training centers. Younie (1966) suggests that screening should insure that:

1. Any physical or emotional problems that might affect work capacity are identified.
2. The child is mature enough to benefit from the program. Age is not always the best guide. His performance in the junior high program is most important and can be used as a screening device.
3. The areas for continued academic work are identified.
4. The degree of parent support is known.
5. The child's social competence level is identified.
6. The level of the child's work interests is known.

This screening is the responsibility of the multi-discipline planning committee of which the vocational guidance counselor has become one of the most important members.

Placement on the job and the necessary follow-up will require a good share of the vocational counselor's time. There are two points of view as to how to handle this problem. The first is that a counselor or counselors should be assigned fulltime to the school-work study program for the mentally retarded and made responsible to the special education director. The second is that the responsibility should be shared by the counselors working in the general education school-work study program. The author favors the second solution as it helps remove the polarization of services and thus helps break down the stigma attached to the mentally retarded.

Role of the Division of Vocational Rehabilitation in the Planning, Counseling, and Placement of the Mentally Retarded

Another monograph in this Series deals with this subject in depth; therefore, only a few summary comments will be made here.

The Office of Vocational Rehabilitation of the U.S. Department of Health, Education, and Welfare has been assigned by law the responsibility for rehabilitating the mentally retarded. It, in turn, has delegated this responsibility to its state Departments or Divisions of Vocational Rehabilitation (DVR). While the responsibility has been long standing, it is only in recent years that the interest and funds have been available for DVR counselors to begin to do an adequate job with the mentally retarded. While considerable progress has been made, there is room for much more to be done.

There are four criteria used in determining eligibility for services by the various Departments or Divisions of Vocational Rehabilitation throughout the country.

1. The applicant must be a resident of the state in which he is applying for help.

2. The applicant must be at or near working age. The minimum is usually 15 years of age.

3. The applicant must have a mental or physical impairment of such severity that it presents a substantial handicap in finding and holding employment.

4. There is a reasonable expectation that the applicant will be employable following rehabilitation services.

For the eligible mentally retarded person the following services are available from DVR. Those marked with an asterisk(*) are available only if they cannot be provided by parents or others.

1. Medical and psychological examinations.

2. Vocational evaluation.

3. Counseling and guidance to determine a suitable vocational objective.

*4. Physical restoration — hospitalization, surgery, artificial appliances, occupational and physical therapy, speech therapy and surgery to remove or reduce a physical impairment.

5. Vocational and adjustment training.

*6. Training and supplies.

*7. Maintenance away from home for training or physical restoration.

8. Assistance in finding a job and follow-up on job.

For more detail on the role of the vocational rehabilitation counselor see Jaques (1970).

Summary

The vocational counseling, planning, and placement of the mentally retarded is a long term process beginning in the elementary school years and continuing through adulthood. It is a process shared by persons skilled in many disciplines, who make up the planning committee for the retarded student. After school age the responsibility shifts to either the Division or Department of Vocational Rehabilitation of his state, whose counselors continue to use a multi-discipline team to help the retarded find a useful, happy life, or to a community center for the retarded with sheltered workshop facilities and services.

The author recognizes that much of what he has included in this chapter only exists in a few advanced school districts; however, he strongly feels that we must strive to make these programs available to all mentally retarded if they are to reach their optimum potential.

5

Needed–A Revolutionary Approach in Rehabilitation of the Mentally Retarded

Since President Kennedy's Panel on Mental Retardation made its report to the nation, there has been a phenomenal increase in interest in the mentally retarded. This has resulted in demands to Congress that something be done to help them — and much has been done in the more spectacular areas. Tremendous amounts of money have been spent for biomedical research to "prevent" mental retardation. For a short time there was great interest and much money spent in such programs as Project Head Start and Upward Bound, though only a small percentage of the mentally retarded were involved in the program. Federal funds were made available to help construct and staff a relatively few community centers for the retarded.

While the percentage of increase in these funds was great, the starting point was so low and the need so great, that only a very small percentage of the retarded have benefited personally from these programs.

The great majority of the retarded, perhaps as many as five and a half million of the estimated six million, need teachers in education and training programs, vocational counselors, and DVR counselors for satisfactory job placement and follow up. They need wide-spread sheltered workshops and work activity centers to give them worthwhile activities to occupy their days. They need direction in the worthwhile use of their leisure time and access to more and better leisure time facilities. Our store of knowledge about the potential of this majority group of the retarded is very limited, yet little is being done in the way of research to learn more about them!

Present Research Emphasis Wrong

Dr. George W. Albee (1968) in a very provocative article stresses the point that most of what is being done today with Federal funds in the areas of research and training is directed towards the minority group of the mentally retarded and not to the majority. He is quoted here at some length because to paraphrase would be to lose the depth of meaning and power of his thought. The author wishes to stress that neither he nor Dr. Albee is attacking the validity of the bio-medical research being done, nor the need for such research; however, both are distressed at the philosophy of disbursement of research funds currently being followed. This philosophy gives the vast majority of research funds to bio-medical research and personnel training facilities, and little to educational-social research and personnel training facilities, thus benefiting the minority of the retarded at the expense of the majority. He states:

> Since 1963, Federal funds for research and training have increased at an unprecedented rate. Unfortunately, most of these funds are not being used to help the majority of the retarded — those who are normally slow, not victims of inherited or acquired diseases. Instead, money is being poured into costly bio-medical research centers and "treatment" clinics to help a minority — those who are retarded because of organic reasons, like injuries, trauma, infections and biochemical imbalances.
>
> The majority of the retarded need not medical treatment but rehabilitative training — so they can use their maximum potential. While every promising research lead should be pursued and every significant effort in the whole field of retardation should be supported, a truly generous part of the new Federal funds ought to be invested in research aimed at helping the retarded lead lives as normal as possible. And, more funds should be spent to train people who will, in turn, help train the majority of the retarded.
>
> At the root of this error in priorities is a tragic misconception — namely, that mental retardation is an inherited or acquired disease.

He continues:

> The truth is that most retardation is not an inherited disease. Quite correctly, President Kennedy's Panel on Mental Retardation emphasized

the fact that '. . . about 75 percent to 85 percent of those now diagnosed as retarded show no demonstrable gross brain abnormality. They are, by and large, persons with relatively mild degrees of retardation . . . Unfavorable environmental and psychological influences are thought to play an important contributory role among this group. Such influences include interference with normal emotional and intellectual stimulation in early infancy, unfavorable psychological emotional experiences in early childhood, and lack of normal intellectual and cultural experiences during the entire developmental period.'

. . .

People are born retarded simply because intelligence is distributed normally throughout the entire population. A certain percentage of all children — slightly more than 2 percent, as it happens — will be born without defect and yet have IQ's below 70. Similarly, a certain percentage — also two percent — will be born with an IQ as high as that of the average graduate student.

. . .

The cold, but realistic fact must be faced. It is no more likely that medical research findings will raise the intelligence of most retardates than it is that research will raise the intelligence of college students.

Let me make it clear that I am not opposing medical research, or deprecating the triumphs of biology and medicine in uncovering the causes of several (albeit rare) forms of retardation in the past decade or so. What I am arguing against is the almost exclusive investment of Federal monies in medically oriented research. For the plain truth is that even after all the post-conception organic causes and all the metabolic and chromosomal defects are discovered and prevented or corrected at least two percent of the general population will still be born retarded. And this situation will prevail for the immediate future.

The problem in trying to get Federal funds for research and training facilities in the social and educational area is the bio-medical orientation of those who control the funds. They have found the funds for the university-affiliated facilities to be a great source for ". . . the academic medical institutions' insatiable need for research money." While there is no question that this research and these facilities are desperately needed in the battle to prevent mental retardation, equally desperate is the need for large amounts of money to be obtained from Congress for research and training facilities in the social-educational area to alleviate the devastating effect of mental retardation on those already born.

The Purdue Achievement Center for Children is an excellent example of how Federal funds, funneled through the state, are being used in the following ways:

1. Service to handicapped children and youth.
2. Service to families of handicapped children and youth.
3. Service to school systems and personnel.
   a. Special diagnostic evaluations.
   b. Special curricula guidance.
   c. Coordinating services of related disciplines in maximizing program services for individual children.
4. Provision of laboratory experiences for students in education and other disciplines concerned with the special needs of children.
5. Provision of practicum experiences for teachers and clinicians in special education and other advanced study courses.
6. Provision of research and program development to the level that present funds will allow.

This grant, amounting to approximately $70,000 per year, provides partial, much needed support for the Special Education program; however, it almost pales into insignificance when compared to the millions of dollars being spent in each of the university-affiliated medical centers.

We have made much in the past of the fact that the mentally retarded are not "sick," that they are not mentally ill. We have carefully distinguished between these two conditions. Yet, the medical vs. the educational-social conflict in programming for the retarded is seen in such insidious ways as renaming state schools as state hospitals, and confusing the public into thinking that the retarded are, perhaps, after all, mentally ill and need "medical treatment."

Dr. Albee states:

> The truth is that 85 percent of the retarded, after thorough medical evaluation, ordinarily require no more medical care than many other handicapped groups in society. The associated physical complications that are correctable, in a majority of cases, are visual and auditory — outside the competence of the ordinary psychiatrist or pediatrician. A significant number of retardates also have speech problems, and these demand the special skills of a speech therapist rather than a physician.
>
> The kind of professional manpower required for effective and functional care of the retarded is not more physicians, nurses, and psychologists, with highly specialized training in this field. These people do not spend any significant amount of their professional time working with the retarded anyway. *More than anything else, we need teachers and vocational-guidance specialists.*

He continues:

> To provide adequate help to the 110,000 children born each year with mild but handicapping retardation, and to provide care and rehabilitation for the other 5,500,000 mildly retarded people in our so-

ciety, we need teachers, teachers, and more teachers — and then taxes to support a massive educational effort. Among teachers in this context I include all those specially trained and devoted professional people willing to spend hours and hours in daily and patient interaction with retarded children unlocking and strengthening whatever skills and abilities are in them. Also included are the vocational rehabilitation workers and those in occupational therapy, in recreation therapy, and in non-professional but patient and warm interaction therapies that the retarded yearn for.

Needed desperately, in addition to teachers, are skilled caseworkers, sheltered-workshop personnel, vocational-guidance counselors, speech therapists, and all the range of other people who have chosen careers that make them their handicapped brother's keeper.

Dr. Albee points out that all of the university-affiliated facilities being built with Federal funds are in medical settings and that few, if any, special educational teachers and vocational counselors will be trained in these facilities.

Where does this lead us? Simply stated, we in education must accept the fact that the education and rehabilitation for the majority of the mentally retarded is an educational problem and that education is going to have to mature to the point of accepting its responsibility. We can no longer abdicate our responsibility. We have been guilty of using medical and psychological terminology and labels, disregarding what this does to the self-concept of the retarded. Education must shake off its lethargy and demand funds to do research in social and educational areas — not sterile empirical research, but applied research, on a large scale that wrestles with topics of effectiveness of various types of programs, new approaches to curriculum, and new techniques of training. These must be massive programs affecting entire school districts and funded for a long enough period of time that the longitudinal effects will be known.

Title III grants under the Elementary, Secondary Education Act started some innovative, massive research projects and programs. However, the three year limitation for funding saw the termination of many of these projects that held promise for opening new doors in programming, if they could have been funded long enough for the long-term effects to become known. True, the local school districts were supposed to pick up these projects, but most districts simply do not have the necessary funds.

As Dr. Albee has so forcefully stated, what is needed is a revolution in the caring for the mentally retarded. The revolution can only come about, however, as educators are awakened to the fact that they have the primary responsibility for these five and a half million retarded who inadvertently are receiving little, if any, help because the professionals who hold the reins have little to offer. Back in 1897, Dr. Maria Montessori, a psychiatrist, decided that the basic program of the retarded was not medical, but educational. Apparently, neither the physicians nor the educators accept her evaluation. Consequently, neither group is doing much for the majority of the retarded.

It is time we educators demand funds to build teaching facilities to train tens of thousands of special educators and vocational guidance counselors. It is time we stop apologizing for not being clinical psychologists or physicians and assume responsibility for applied educational research and more applied educational research. It is time we train educational researchers to look beyond a sterile research design to see what can be made to happen with and to the whole child. It is time we throw out the idea that there are those we cannot educate and find out why we have not been doing so.

School counselors are in an ideal position to carry out applied educational research in all phases of assessment and education, program planning, counseling, placement, and follow-up of the mentally retarded. Everything that they try should be reported. Failure is just as important to the total store of knowledge as is success.

The school counselor working with the special education teachers and the DVR counselor can carry out longitudinal studies with retarded children. The cost would be small, the investment in time not great, but the results could be shocking to the status quo.

Needed — New Concepts in Employment of Mentally Retarded

In our philosophy of employment of the retarded, we have taken the first step of a thousand mile journey. The movement of the Federal government into the employment of the mentally retarded in Civil Service jobs was truly a breakthrough; however, it is only a token of what could be.

At every level of government, job analysis should be made of minimum requirements for all jobs within the range of the mentally retarded and a specified number of these held open to be filled only by the retarded. One of the major stumbling blocks to this plan is that many of the jobs that could be filled by the retarded come under the heading of political patronage. This is a sacred cow that will be difficult to overcome.

In every department of local, state, and federal government there are jobs the retarded could fill. The majority of the mildly retarded could be placed in useful employment and become tax payers rather than tax consumers.

The school counselor can join with the DVR counselors in placing the request before the various levels of government to open a number of these positions for their school-work study retarded — especially for employment after graduating.

Needed — Revolution in the Rehabilitation of the Mentally Retarded

The National Association for Retarded Children in its publication "Facts of Mental Retardation," has concisely stated thirteen steps urgently required to meet the needs of the retarded. The author has re-ordered these steps in line with his feeling that a revolution is needed in the areas of research, training of personnel, and development of educational vocational training, placement and follow-up programs, if the majority of the mentally retarded are to benefit. If these steps were taken, a revolution would truly occur in the rehabilitation of the mentally retarded. (The numbers in parentheses indicate original order.)

(2) 1. Research in the behavioral and social sciences relevant to prevention of socio-cultural forms of mental retardation, and relevant to techniques of training and management which will more effectively develop the fullest potentials of which each retarded individual is capable.

(1) 2. Research in bio-medical fields relevant to prevention and treatment.

(3) 3. Orientation of physicians to the early diagnosis and positive management of mentally retarded youngsters in their care.

(4) 4. Extension of public health nursing services to provide practical assistance to mothers in the everyday problems of rearing a retarded child.

(6) 5. Extension of public school programs for the educable and trainable, especially in those states which have heretofore provided inadequate legislative and financial bases for these programs.

(7) 6. Recruitment and effective training of some 50,000 new teachers. [Added to this should be thousands of specially trained vocational guidance counselors needed for effective school-work study programs.]

(5) 7. The extension of specialized diagnostic facilities [expanding these facilities to provide specific, individualized training programs as well as diagnosis] so that they are reasonably accessible to all population groups in all parts of the country.

(8) 8. Development of improvement techniques of selective placement of the mildly retarded youth and adult in gainful em-

ployment tied with interpretation to employers of the assets and limitations of the retarded employee.

(9) 9. Extension and improvement of opportunities for sheltered employment of those incapable of entering the competitive employment market.

(10)10. Modification of laws governing the civil status of the mentally retarded.

(11)11. New approaches to protective services, guardianship, social guidance, and economic security for the retarded adult who cannot contribute substantially to his own support.

(12)12. Development of diversified residential facilities close to the main stream of community life and professional service, and adapted to the various individual needs apparent among the retarded children and adults in need of residential care.

(13)13. Effective planning and coordination of major public and private activities at national, regional, state, and local levels.

The imbalance in research and training funding is reflected in the original ordering of these steps or perhaps grows out of this order. As Dr. Albee has pointed out, the most vocal parents supporting the biomedical research emphasis are those whose children tend to be in the minority group of the retarded.

Issues to be Faced in Effecting the Revolution in Rehabilitation

The President's Committee on Mental Retardation (1967) in making its first report on progress made in combating mental retardation listed ten areas urgently needing attention. Each of these areas deserves special consideration; however, the tenth area gives us much to think about. It is stated as follows: "Lastly, we urge that everyone interested in helping the mentally retarded and combating retardation give thought to imaginative ideas and approaches that will make new advances possible." The Committee then posed several questions on which "bold, original thinking and ideas are needed . . .":

> What is the cost to the nation of mental retardation? That cost is known to be staggering in terms of service expenditure and undeveloped human resource. Its more precise determination and elaboration in terms of long-term national societal trends is a major planning need.
>
> With jobs being increasingly designed for people, what kinds of job engineering can and need to be done for the retarded? What kind of teaching-training techniques need to be designed for use with the retarded to ready them for jobs designed for their particular skills?
>
> In the increasingly complex city, how shall we at once utilize and protect those mentally retarded who can support themselves in a job but need a form of guardianship in their off-duty hours?

How shall we plan to serve the mentally retarded among the 10 percent of the U.S. population who will continue to live in small towns and rural areas?

What will shorter work weeks and more leisure time for Americans generally mean for the retarded? Will there be adequate volunteer help available? What of recreation for the retarded themselves — what are its undiscovered potentials for bringing the retarded a greater share in the fullness of daily life? How shall wè inspire young America to enter this critically important field, both as volunteers and as career workers?

What job, personnel and career changes and innovations will be necessary to match available skills and resources to the meeting of ever-growing need in the mental retardation field?

What are the moral and ethical implications of technological findings in the genetics and management of mental retardation? Should a discourse on these subjects be instituted among scientists, philosophers, theologians, social theorists, parents?

Because the counselor must be interested and involved in the total problem, these questions are listed for his consideration and hopefully for action.

Guidance and the Mentally Retarded Student

This monograph has attempted to present the case for the rehabilitation of the mentally retarded student. Areas in which the author felt the school counselor could make a vital contribution to the rehabilitation process were pointed out. Ideal situations were described in an effort to point out what should be, rather than concentrating on the dismal side of what too frequently is allowed to exist. Hopefully, the school counselor will "get involved" in this revolution that is taking place to help the mentally retarded find the dignity that they deserve as human beings.

Massive education of the public to the desperate needs of the mentally retarded is the only way to bring about the needed revolution successfully. In your position you can be one of the most valuable friends of the retarded person.

Client Referral Procedure

The Fort Wayne State Hospital and Training Center and the Indiana Vocational Rehabilitation Division will work cooperatively for those individuals judged mentally retarded and suitable for vocational diagnostic services or vocational training. To aid in determining procedural steps and establishment of a consistent process, two methods of referral will be utilized. Also included in this Appendix are four sample forms used during the rehabilitation process: (1) Job Classification, (2) Job Description, (3) Work Evaluation Report, and (4) Terminal Report.

I. *Clients referred from Indiana Vocational Rehabilitation Division to Fort Wayne State Hospital and Training Center.*

    A. The Vocational Rehabilitation Division counselor from the Indiana Vocational Rehabilitation Division will be responsible for initial screening of clients in determining eligibility. This procedure will include: (1) filing of an application for services, (2) completion of a general medical examination, (3) psychological assessment of intelligence and vocational aptitudes, and (4) contact with the client's family to determine their willingness for client's admission to Fort Wayne State Hospital and Training Center on a voluntary admission basis.

    B. When all the procedural materials have been assembled and eligibility has been determined, the Vocational Rehabilitation Division counselor will contact and forward all information on the prospective client to the liaison counselor at the Ginsberg Rehabilitation Center. At the time of contact and forwarding of information, the Vocational Rehabilitation Division counselor will indicate the types of services needed by his client (assessment, work evaluation, work adjustment, on-the-job training, etc.). This information is necessary for determining length of admission to the Training Center and program planning.

C. When all required information has been received by the liaison counselor, this material is reviewed by the Admissions Committee. The responsibility of this committee is to review the referral material, determine feasibility of the client for program services, and establish an admission date. The membership of this committee is composed of the Unit Administrator, the social worker from Ginsberg Rehabilitation Center, the liaison counselor, the workshop supervisor, the Director of Psychological Services, and the regional (county) social worker from the Department of Social Services. If applicable, representatives from other disciplines and agencies may be invited to participate as needs of individual clients may warrant. This may include the local Vocational Rehabilitation Division counselor.

D. The liaison counselor is responsible for contacting the client's Vocational Rehabilitation Division counselor in reference to the recommendations from the admissions committee. If admission is recommended, an admission date will be provided.

E. If necessary, the regional (county) social worker from the Social Services Department will assist the Vocational Rehabilitation Division counselor and the Ginsberg Rehabilitation Team by working with the family, gathering information, providing relevant materials, etc.

F. The social worker from Ginsberg Rehabilitation Center will be responsible for the procedures leading to admission to the Training Center. This will include application for admission, contacting record offices, etc.

G. As the client is scheduled through the program phases, the liaison counselor will be responsible for assembling and forwarding progress reports to the Vocational Rehabilitation Division counselors. The liaison counselor will be responsible for notifying the Vocational Rehabilitation Division counselor as to the determined vocational objective, the total rehabilitation plan, and the approximate date of completing the program, (the earliest possible date).

H. At the termination date, the Social Worker from Ginsberg Rehabilitation Center is responsible for discharging the client from the Training Center. The client will be returned to his respective community under the supervision of the Vocational Rehabilitation Division counselor for job placement. Suggestions for an individual's entry into job placements will be correlated with the Dictionary of Occupational Titles.

I. The liaison counselor will be responsible for assembling and forwarding all final progress reports to the Vocational Rehabilitation Division counselor.

J. The regional (county) social worker from the Social Services Department may be in contact with the client through community agencies, family, Vocational Rehabilitation Division counselor, etc., in helping to make community adjustment.

II. *Clients referred from Fort Wayne State Hospital and Training Center to the Indiana Vocational Rehabilitation Division.*

A. The liaison counselor from the Ginsberg Rehabilitation Center is responsible for (1) completing an application for prospective clients, (2) scheduling for general medical examination, and (3) scheduling for psychological assessment of intelligence and vocational aptitudes.

B. The liaison counselor is responsible for contacting the Division of Vocational Rehabilitation, Fort Wayne Office, and forwarding all necessary information to the respective counselor, (the Fort Wayne office is staffed by three (3) counselors who are responsible for clients listed in alphabetical order in Allen County only).

C. The Vocational Rehabilitation Division counselor is responsible for signing all Vocational Rehabilitation Division forms and determining acceptance of client for services. If a client is accepted, the Vocational Rehabilitation Division counselor will contact the liaison counselor as to the type of vocational services desired.

D. The social worker from the Ginsberg Rehabilitation Center is responsible for notifying the client's family, the regional social worker from Social Services Department and other participating disciplines in reference to the vocational training plans.

E. As the client is scheduled through the program phases, the liaison counselor is responsible for assembling and forwarding progress reports to the Vocational Rehabilitation Division counselor. The liaison counselor is responsible for notifying the Vocational Rehabilitation Division counselor on the vocational objective determined and the approximate date of completing the program, (at the earliest possible date).

F. At the termination date of program services, the client will be referred back to the Vocational Rehabilitation Division counselor for placement or continued training at another facility. Several weeks before the completion of the training program, a determination must be made as to the type of job the client will be best equipped to perform. Suggestions for an individual's entry into job placement will be correlated with the Dictionary of Occupational Titles. This will enable all concerned parties to locate suitable employment.

FORT WAYNE STATE HOSPITAL AND TRAINING CENTER
GINSBERG REHABILITATION UNIT
JOB CLASSIFICATION CORRELATED TO D.O.T.

Job Classification	Dishwasher, Machine
DOT Code	3-18.887
	Service
	Kitchen Worker
	Handling

Worker Trait Components	Code	Requirements
General Education Development		
Reasoning:	2	Apply common sense to carry out instructions from standardized situations.
Mathematical:		
Language:	1	Learn job from oral instruction and/or short demonstration.
Specific Vocational Preparation:	2	Short demonstration up to and including 30 days.
Interests:	1	Preference for dealing with things and objects.
	3	Activities of a routine, concrete, organized nature.
Physical Demands:	1	20 pounds maximum, frequently 10 pounds
	1	Reaching-extending the hands and arms in any direction.
	6	Seeing-clarity of vision at 10 feet or less.
Temperaments:	2	Short, repetitive operations carried out according to set procedures.
	3	Little room for independent judgment.
Aptitudes		
Intelligence:	5	Lowest 10% of the population
Verbal:	5	Lowest 10% of the population
Numerical:	5	Lowest 10% of the population
Spatial:	4	Lower 33% of the population excluding the bottom 10%
Form Perception:	4	Lower 33% of the population excluding the bottom 10%
Clerical Perception:	5	Lowest 10% of the population

Motor Coordination:	4	Lower 33% of the population excluding the bottom 10%
Finger Dexterity:	4	Lower 33% of the population excluding the bottom 10%
Manual Dexterity:	4	Lower 33% of the population excluding the bottom 10%
Eye-Hand-Foot Coordination:	5	Lowest 10% of the population
Color Discrimination:	5	Lowest 10% of the population

Working Conditions:	1	Inside
	2	Humid
		atmospheric condition with high moisture content

Dictionary of Occupational Titles
  Related Classifications:

<u>Group</u>

Manipulating	.884	P. 322
Tending	.885	P. 447
Feeding-offbearing	.886	P. 356

FORT WAYNE STATE HOSPITAL AND TRAINING CENTER
GINSBERG REHABILITATION UNIT
JOB DESCRIPTION

DOT Description

Performs any combination of the following duties to maintain kitchen work
areas and restaurant equipment and utensils in clean and orderly condition:
Sweeps and mops floors. Washes worktables, walls, refrigerators, and meat
blocks. Segregates and removes trash and garbage and places in designated
containers. Steam-cleans or hoses-out garbage cans. Sorts bottles and
breaks disposable ones in bottle-crushing machine. Washes pots, pans, and
trays by hand. Scrapes food from dishes and washes them by hand or places
them in racks or on conveyor to dishwashing machine. Places silver in revolving burnishing-machine tumbler, dips it in chemical solutions, holds it
against buffing wheel, and rubs it with cloth to remove tarnish and restore
luster. Holds inverted glasses over revolving brushes to clean inside sur-
faces. Transfers supplies and equipment between storage and work areas by
hand or by use of handtruck. Sets up banquet tables. Washes and peels
vegetables, using knife or peeling machine.

FWSH & TC Application:

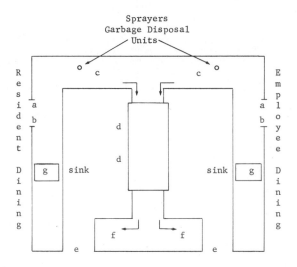

(Employee on duty at all times - the resident need not know how to add
detergent; start-stop machine)

As residents finish eating, they place their trays on the counter (through
the opening on their side of the scullery). Some residents will take the
paper off their trays and place in a container outside the scullery, may
place their drinking container in a dishwashing rack at a, and place their
silverware in the rack at b. When the resident does not do these functions,
the employee (or working resident) must segregate the paper, utensils, and
drinking containers.

After everything has been taken off the tray, except food and food particles, the trays are pushed over the counter to the person working at the sprayer. This person empties as much of the food as possible off the tray and into the garbage disposal unit and then sprays the tray (both sides) to remove the remaining pieces. The trays are placed in a rack at c and when the rack is full, it is pushed into the washer. (The trays are placed in the racks all the same way.) The trays are placed on their sides, the large compartment up, and the food side is pushed in the washer at the front. The drinking containers are placed opening down. When a tray containing either the drinking containers or silverware is full, the employee carries it to the washer and inserts it to be washed. (Certain utensils, silverware, etc., may have to be washed before a rack is full if a shortage occurs in the dining area).

Besides the actual pieces used in the resident dining hall, food containers and dishes used elsewhere (feeding the babies, etc.) are washed here. These are either brought in or gotten from assigned areas, sprayed, racked, and washed as the other equipment.

The machine pulls the racks through the dishwasher. The racks are started in at the entrance end and after approximately 55 seconds, will push at least halfway out at the exit. Residents need not reach into the machine for the racks. The doors on the side of the machine at d should not be opened while water is running in the machine. This water is 180 degrees F. Working residents eat at 10:30 a.m. Other residents and employees at 11:00.

When the racks come out of the washer, they are pulled around to the work area at f:

    Trays: The trays are shaken or hit on the edge of the rack to remove excess water and are stacked in the bus at e. The racks are pushed toward the doors at d so when an employee at c is ready, he or she need only to turn around for another rack. When needed, trays are bussed to the dining area.

    Silverware: The silverware is segregated and placed in plastic containers as to kind. Residents eating in the hall may come for the containers if they are short on the serving line.

    Drinking Containers: The drinking containers are also bussed to the dining area. Racks for silverware and drinking containers are pushed toward a & b. These racks are also used when washing food containers from upstairs.

    Resident equipment: Employee:

        White glasses   Blue cups
        Colored trays except blue   Yellow glasses
                                   Blue trays

The operation on the employee side is almost the same with the following exceptions:

The worker must segregate all silverware, paper, and drinking containers. Silverware, cups, glasses, salad bowls, etc. are rinsed in the sink at g before being placed in the washer.

FORT WAYNE STATE HOSPITAL AND TRAINING CENTER
GINSBERG REHABILITATION UNIT
PHASE II WORK EVALUATION

Name___Smith, John_____   Referring Agency___Vocational Rehabilitation___

Testing Period__2-24-69___ to __3-4-69___   Referral Made by_____

Explanation: Each client is administered a battery of twenty-two work sample tasks. The battery of tasks are developmental in nature and are reported in three levels. A normal individual will probably score between 95% and 105% on these tests. The competency of the retarded client will be reflected in the scores the client obtains, the higher the score the greater degree of competency.

For example, if a client would score 90% on level one, 85% on level two, and 70% on level three, the findings would indicate this client is ready vocationally for placement in the community. The vocational placement should consist of a simpler, repetitious job with initial close supervision. This client would have excellent potential to be upgraded into more complex jobs with lesser supervision required.

Overall Test Results___93%___

LEVEL I   Capable of institutional work or possibly sheltered workshop setting. Simple repetitive work, close structured supervision needed. Average percent scored __94__

This client is considered a very heavy worker, lifting and carrying abilities up to 120 pounds. Probably could work throughout the day lifting and carrying 70 to 80 pounds. No physical limitations. He has excellent manipulation of small objects. He can accurately follow a sequence of order on a simple repetitive one and two step operation assembly. He can handle hand tools efficiently.

LEVEL II   Community potential, repetitive work of three to four step sequential operation. Needs initial close supervision, but can be upgraded to moderate supervision within a short training period. Average percent scored __95__

This client can accurately match abstract items on a one to one relationship. Performed in the range of normal on the assembly of a mechanical parts test. Is sensitive to various weights and can judge material as to volume. He can follow sequence of order on a repetitious task with accuracy. Performed within the range of normal on a test using a drill press in which a client is asked to drill 250 holes accurately.

LEVEL III   Excellent community possibilities--varied job situations--in which simple to average problem solving abilities can be employed. Generally reliable. From a vocational point the client can operate close to an average worker. Average percent scored __90__

This client should be scheduled for work on this level. He has abilities to perform work sample tasks involving problem solving of a simple nature at first, progressing to more complex problem solving situations. Progression would depend upon the attitude of the client in the particular job. This ' client can work well in a machine controlled situation. His eye-hand coordination is excellent and he works quickly with the use of his hands. Good arm pressure control. Has fair inspection abilities with fair discrimination. The weakness in this area was due to carelessness.

JUDGMENTAL FACTORS

Explanation: This is a subjective analysis of the motivational factor during the testing period. These observations were made by the evaluator and observed from a vocational standpoint.

Positive	Unable to judge	Negative		Comments: John was very cooperative throughout the testing period. This tester feels he was working up to his abilities. He showed an interest in his work but was bored at times by simpler, repetitious type work. At times, he gave the impression that he thought some of the tasks were child's play.
x			Willingness to work	
x			Working up to abilities	
x			Capable of accurate performance	
x			Shows interest in work	
x			Listening abilities	

JOB POSSIBILITIES: Based on abilities, interest and vocational functioning level of the client. Also job availabilities in the home community are taken into consideration. (Excluded in this case)

This client's abilities lie in the area of Feeding-Offbearing of machines as defined by the Dictionary of Occupational Titles. He has good manual and finger dexterity and has an expressed interest in the field of mechanics. His vocational functioning level is such that he can be rated in the realm of an average worker. If jobs are not available in the Feeding-Offbearing area, John could efficiently perform jobs in the areas of manipulation and handling if they were challenging to him.

Job suggestion for entry level would include the following:

1. burr grinder
2. machine feeder
3. welding-machine feeder
4. tire trimming-machine feeder

5. mill operator-helper
6.. polishing machine operator-helper
7. packaging laborer
8. spray unit feeder

VOCATIONAL WEAKNESSES:

It is the opinion of the workshop staff that this client has excellent potential; the only weakness we have observed in the past two months is one of attitude. He likes to give the impression of being self-assured. We feel the two main reasons for this false front are his chronological age of 17 and the poor home situation from which he came.

BEHAVIORAL OBSERVATIONS: Includes interpersonal relationships of supervisor and peers.

This client appeared to be bored with the monotony of repetitious tasks. He was very cooperative and had good self expression. He had adequate sociability with his peers and the supervisor in the workshop setting.   He had the ability to work without supervision and guidance.   He had neat appearance and was motivated in tasks that challenged him.   He performed at a consistent rate of speed.   He had no hesitation when beginning something new and his perseverance was good.   He was reliable in terms of attendance and punctuality.

SUGGESTIONS: Continue to work adjustment:

Workshop - build up production capacity, discourage "cocky" attitude, encourage realistic attitude
Classes - academics, community orientation, and industrial arts
Counseling - aid and support client in attitude problem
Community placement - part-time work

SUMMARY: John has the ability and interest to do an excellent job in a factory setting.   He is going to need continual support to overcome his feelings of uncertainty.   However, the young age of this client is a positive factor in overcoming this attitude problem.

FORT WAYNE STATE HOSPITAL
AND
TRAINING CENTER

TERMINAL REPORT

4-22-69

Doe, Joe

Joe was referred to the Ginsberg Rehabilitation Center on October 21, 1968 from the Gary office of the Vocational Rehabilitation Division. Psychological reports included in the referral described Joe as being "a self-depressed individual both emotionally and intellectually," who "lacks the mental ability to develop skills, either academic or vocational, that would permit him to function without supervision." A psychiatric report indicated that Joe was "almost completely disabled as a depressed young man."

Projective tests given during the Assessment and Planning Phase indicated that, although Joe tried to be cooperative, this was superficial and he was quite passively resistive. Joe was programmed through two phases and on the results of the Vocational, Leisure Time, and Education testing showed that he functioned above the norms established by the population of Ginsberg. He was placed on a part-time job at a restaurant on weekends and participated in the Work Adjustment program in the Simulated Workshop during the week. Joe's employer at the restaurant found that he required little supervision and needed to be given directions only once. He offered Joe a full-time job there but the staff felt a more demanding job that required a higher level of functioning would be more appropriate.

On December 18, 1968, Joe was returned home with the idea of obtaining a job. He was unable to do so and his interpersonal relations with his mother were extremely poor. Joe returned to Ginsberg Rehabilitation Center on February 7, 1969. During the next week he was placed at a Car Wash. He continued to work in this setting and the employer was extremely pleased with his performance. He told the community vocational counselor that, "I wish for 10 more workers just like Joe." The employer thinks so highly of Joe that he put him on a guaranteed 40 hour week and pays even on days when it rains and he can't work.

Joe was moved to the Halfway House on March 15, 1969, where he could be able to practice the responsibilities of independent living. The Halfway House supervisor has reported that Joe has adjusted well to this move and is using community recreation facilities extensively. Joe has learned a great deal about managing money since this move was initiated. He buys his own meals and clothing, pays rent, and saves money out of his checks to take the bus home for occasional visits.

In summary, this is a 17 year old boy who came to the Ginsberg Rehabilitation Center with the prognosis that he would never be able to function without supervision. He now presents a picture of a well adjusted, likable young man who is functioning very well in a semi-independent setting. The staff feels that he can be discharged to independent community living this summer and be able to be a contributing member of society.

National Organizations
Interested in Mental Retardation

1. *International Council for Exceptional Children* (C.E.C.)
   Address: 1201 16th Street, N.W.
   Washington 6, D.C.
   Purpose: The organization was established to further professional growth of those working with exceptional children, and to serve as a source of information for allied professions and the public in hopes that the needs of the exceptional child may be better served.
   Divisions Interested in Mental Retardation:
   a) Division of Mental Retardation
   b) Council for Children with Behavioral Disorders
   c) Council for Administrators of Special Education
   d) Council for Children with Learning Disorders
   Publications: Journal entitled *Exceptional Children,* published 10 months a year.
2. *American Association on Mental Deficiency* (A.A.M.D.)
   Address: 5201 Connecticut Avenue, N.W.
   Washington, D.C. 20015
   Purpose: A professional organization dedicated to the welfare of the mentally deficient, those who work with them, and the concern for the field in general. Also seeks continuous development of professional staff and encourages research in the field of mental deficiency.

Divisions: Divided into 12 geographical regions and the following professional divisions:

Administration	Social Work
Religion	General
Medicine	Cottage & Ward Life
Nursing	Recreation
Physical Therapy	Speech Path. & Aud.
Psychology	Voc. Rehab.
Education	

Publications: *American Journal of Mental Deficiency* — Bi-monthly *Mental Retardation* — Bi-monthly

3. *American Speech & Hearing Association* (A.S.H.A.)

Address: 1001 Connecticut Avenue
Washington, D.C.

Purpose: Professional growth of members and concern with welfare of speech and hearing handicapped.

Publications: *Journal of Speech and Hearing Disorders — Clinical Research Quarterly* A.S.H.A. — Monthly publication

4. *National Association for Retarded Children* (N.A.R.C.)

Address: 420 Lexington Avenue
New York, N.Y. 10017

Purpose: A non-profit organization of parents and friends organized to promote the welfare of the mentally retarded child.

Publications: *Children Unlimited* — Bi-monthly newspaper

5. *Association for Children with Learning Disabilities* (A.C.L.D.)

Address: 2200 Brownsville Road
Pittsburgh, Pa. 15210

Purpose: To advance the education and general well-being of children with normal, potentially normal, or above average intelligence who have learning disabilities arising from perceptual, conceptual or subtle coordinative problems, sometimes accompanied by behavioral difficulties.

Publications: Newsletter

6. *American Personnel & Guidance Association* (A.P.G.A.)

Address: 1605 New Hampshire Avenue, N.W.
Washington, D.C. 20009

Purpose: To advance the scientific discipline of personnel and guidance work, to conduct and foster programs of education in the field of personnel and guidance, to promote sound professional practices and to publish scientific, educational and professional literature.

Publications: *Personnel and Guidance Journal* — (10 issues a year)
Divisions Interested in Mental Retardation:

a) *American Rehabilitation Counseling Association* (A.R.C.A.)
   Address: 1605 New Hampshire Avenue, N.W.
      Washington, D.C. 20009
   Purpose: To foster rehabilitation counseling — encourage research and development of men, materials, and ideas. To establish standards of professional services in the area.
   Publications: *The Rehabilitation Counseling Bulletin* — Quarterly

b) *National Vocational Guidance Association* (N.V.G.A.)
   Address: 1605 New Hampshire Avenue, N.W.
      Washington, D.C. 20009
   Purpose: To foster vocational guidance and occupational adjustment and to establish and improve standards of professional services in these fields.
   Publications: Vocational Guidance Quarterly

c) *American School Counselors Association* (A.S.C.A.)
   Address: 1605 New Hampshire Avenue, N.W.
      Washington, D.C. 20009
   Purpose: To broaden and deepen counselors' knowledge in the many areas encompassed by guidance and counseling, which in turn helps them to serve youth better.
   Publications: *School Counselor* — quarterly, and Newsletter

7. *National Rehabilitation Association* (N.R.A.)
   Address: 1025 Vermont Avenue, N.W.
      Washington, D.C.
   Purpose: Advance rehabilitation for all physically and mentally handicapped persons by fostering research, developing professional standards, providing publications and conferences, and increasing public understanding.
   Publications: *Journal of Rehabilitation* and Newsletter — Monthly

8. *National Association of Sheltered Workshops & Homebound Programs, Inc.*
   Address: 1029 Vermont Avenue, N.W.
      Washington, D.C.
   Purpose: To train retarded children in the fundamentals of competitive employment. In most cases the workshop serves as a transition between special class in the public schools and competitive employment.
   Publications: Quarterly bulletin to members

9. *United Cerebral Palsy Association* (U.C.P.)
   Address: 321 West 44th Street
      New York, New York
   Purpose: To work through established agencies to improve treat-

ment facilities, training, education and recreation for cerebral palsied children, adults and their families. To provide services for individuals such as braces and other equipment. Also to provide funds for post-graduate training and other specialized training for technicians in the treatment of cerebral palsy.

Publications: *The Crusader* — Monthly

10. *National Society for Crippled Children and Adults*

Address: 2023 West Ogden Avenue
   Chicago, Illinois

Purpose: To engage in activities to improve health, welfare, education, rehabilitation, employment and recreation facilities and opportunities for crippled children and adults, regardless of age, race, religion, or economic status.

Publications: Annual report, Quarterly Easter Seal bulletins

11. *American Psychological Association* (A.P.A.)

Address: 1200 17th Street, N.W.
   Washington, D.C.

Purpose: To advance psychology as a science and as a means of promoting human welfare. It attempts to further these objectives by holding annual meetings, publishing psychological journals, and working toward improved standards for psychological training and service.

Divisions Interested in Mental Retardation:

a) Division of Clinical Psychology (XII)
b) Division of Educational Psychology (XV)
c) Division of School Psychologists (XVI)
d) Division of Counseling Psychology (XVII)
e) Division of Psychological Aspects of Disability (XXII)
f) Division of Experimental Analysis of Behavior (XXV)

Publications: *American Psychologist* — Monthly, plus divisional journals.

....

Referral Agencies for the Mentally Retarded Within a Typical State

Most of the following agencies are located within the state of Indiana; however, most states have similar agencies who work with the retarded. More detailed information on these agencies may be found in the *Directory of Services for the Handicapped* developed by the Commission for the Handicapped, Indiana State Board of Health. Copies of this directory may be obtained from the Commission, 1330 W. Michigan Street, Indianapolis, Ind. 46202.

1. Achievement Center for Children — Purdue University
   Address: Stanley Coulter Annex, Room 101, Purdue University, West Lafayette, Ind. 47906
2. Gateway Learning Center
   Address: 300 East Adams Street, Franklin, Ind. 46131
3. Gateway School
   Address: 211 Gateway Drive, Peru, Ind. 46970
4. Green Acres
   Address: 800 Mendleson Drive, Richmond, Ind. 47374
5. Harrison County Crusade School for Retarded Children, Inc.
   Address: Palmyra, Ind. 47164
6. Indiana Department of Mental Health
   Address: 1315 West 10th Street, Indianapolis, Ind. 46202

7. Indiana State Board of Health
   Address: 1330 West Michigan Street, Indianapolis, Ind. 46202
8. Indiana State Department of Public Instruction — Division of Special Education
   Address: Room 223, State House, Indianapolis, Ind. 46204
9. Indiana University Medical Center
   Address: 1100 West Michigan Street, Indianapolis, Ind. 46207
10. James Whitcomb Riley Memorial Association
    Address: 129 East Market Street, Indianapolis, Ind. 46204
11. Johnny Appleseed School and Training Center
    Address: 2542 Thompson, Fort Wayne, Ind. 46807
12. Joseph Rauch Center for the Retarded
    Address: Abbydell & Shrader Avenues, New Albany, Ind. 47150
13. Lake County Association for Retarded Children, Inc.
    Address: 2702 W. 35th Avenue, Gary, Ind. 46408
14. Lake County Children's Home
    Address: 2316 Jefferson Street, Gary, Ind. 46407
15. Lake County Mental Health Clinic
    Address: 4801 West 5th Avenue, Gary, Ind. 46406
16. Marian Day School for Retarded Children
    Address: 1614 Glendale, Evansville, Ind. 47712
17. Logan School and Center for the Mentally Retarded
    Address: 2228 E. Colfax Avenue, South Bend, Ind. 46615
18. Opportunity Center, Incorporated
    Address: 1015 Third Street, Columbus, Ind. 47201
19. Opportunity Cottage Training Center for Retarded Children
    Address: Box 372-A, R. R. 2, Danville, Ind. 46122
20. Opportunity Industries, Inc.
    Address: 2715 South Western Avenue, Marion, Ind. 46952
21. Opportunity School
    Address: Box 264, Columbia City, Ind. 46725
22. Opportunity School
    Address: 818 East Harrison Street, Rensselaer, Ind. 47978
23. Opportunity School for Retarded Children
    Address: 1620 West 7th Street, Anderson, Ind. 46011
24. Our Lady of Mercy Hospital-Sanitarium
    Address: U.S. Highway 30, Dyer, Ind. 46311
25. The Rehabilitation Center
    Address: 702 Williams Street, Elkhart, Ind. 46514
26. The Rehabilitation Center, Inc.
    Address: 3701 Bellmeade Avenue, Evansville, Ind. 47715
27. Rosemary Kennedy School
    Address: 3 East Walnut Street, Washington, Ind. 47501

28. State Hospitals and Training Centers for the Retarded
    Fort Wayne State Hospital and Training Center
    801 East State Boulevard, Fort Wayne, Ind. 46805
    Muscatatuck State Hospital and Training Center
    Butlerville, Ind. 47223
    Northern Indiana Children's Hospital
    1234 North Notre Dame Avenue, South Bend, Ind. 46622
29. Sunshine School for Retarded Children
    Address: 321 East 16th Street, Seymour, Ind. 47274
30. School of Hope
    Address: Box 211, Wabash, Ind. 46992
31. Shelbyville Workshop, Inc.
    Address: 157 East Broadway, Shelbyville, Ind. 46176
32. Sheltered Workshop
    Address: 624 South Jefferson Street, Muncie, Ind. 47305
33. Therapy Center for Retarded Children of LaPorte County
    Address: 3200 Cleveland Avenue, Michigan City, Ind. 46360
34. Tippecanoe County Mental Health Center, Inc.
    Address: 2900 North River Road, West Lafayette, Ind. 47906
35. Trainable Class
    Address: Boys Club Building, Riley Park, Greenfield, Ind. 46140
36. The Volunteers of America
    Address: 422 North Capitol Avenue, Indianapolis, Ind. 46204
37. Wabash Center for the Mentally Retarded, Inc.
    Address: 2000 Greenbush Street, Lafayette, Ind. 47904
38. Wee Haven Industries
    Address: Box 233, Garrett, Ind. 46738
39. Wee Haven School
    Address: Box 233, Garrett, Indiana 46738
40. West Lake County Center
    Address: 3800 Grand Avenue E., Chicago, Illinois 46312

BIBLIOGRAPHY

Albee, George W., "Needed — A Revolution in Caring for the Retarded." *Trans-Action*, Vol. 5, 1968, pp. 37–42.

Anderson, R., *The Child with Learning Disabilities and Guidance.* Boston: Houghton Mifflin Co., 1970.

Blackman, L. W., & Siperstein, G. N., "Job Analysis and the Vocational Evaluation of the Mentally Retarded." *Rehabilitation Lit.*, Vol. 29, 1968, pp. 103–105.

Blatt, B., "Toward a More Acceptable Terminology in Mental Retardation." *Training School Bulletin*, Vol. 58, 1961, pp. 47–57.

Campanelle, T. C., *Counseling Parents of Mentally Retarded Children.* Milwaukee: The Bruce Publishing Co., 1965.

Cruickshank, W. M., *A Teaching Method for Brain Injured and Hyperactive Children.* Syracuse, N.Y.: Syracuse University, 1961.

Dillon, E. J., Heath, E. J., & Biggs, C. W., *Comprehension Developmental Programming for Success in Learning.* Columbus, Ohio: Charles E. Merrill Books, 1970.

Doll, E. A., "The Essentials of an Inclusive Concept of Mental Deficiency." *Amer. J. Ment. Defic.*, Vol. 46, 1941, pp. 214–219.

Faust, V., *Establishing Guidance Programs in Elementary Schools.* Boston: Houghton Mifflin Co., 1968.

Frostig, Marianne, & Home, D., *The Frostig Program for the Development of Visual Perception.* Chicago: Follett, 1964.

Gallendar, D., and others, *Grant Proposal Ginsberg Rehabilitation Unit at Fort Wayne State Hospital and Training Center with Indiana State Department of Vocational Rehabilitation (Section II Funds).* Unpublished proposal submitted to Indiana Division of Vocational Rehabilitation, Nov. 1967.

Heath, E. J., "Field Trips for Life Experiences." *Ment. Retard.*, June 1966, pp. 42–43.

———, and others, *Proposal for Establishment of Rehabilitation Facilities at Fort Wayne State School under the Hill-Burton Program* (Public Law 482). Unpublished proposal submitted to U.S. Department of Health, Education, and Welfare, Oct. 1962.

Heber, R. A., "A Manual on Terminology and Classifications in Mental Retardation." *Amer. J. Ment. Defic.*, Vol. 44, 1959, Monog. Suppl.

———, "Modifications in the Manual on Terminology and Classification in Mental Retardation." *Amer. J. Ment. Defic.*, Vol. 45, 1961, pp. 499–500.

Hutt, M. L., & Gibby, R. G., *The Mentally Retarded Child: Development, Education and Treatment* (2nd ed.). Boston: Allyn & Bacon, 1965.

Jaques, Marceline E., *Vocational Rehabilitation Counseling and Services.* Boston: Houghton Mifflin Co., 1970.

Jordan, T. E., *The Mentally Retarded* (2nd ed.). Columbus, Ohio: Charles E. Merrill Books, 1966.

Kephart, N.C., *Learning Disabilities: An Educational Adventure. West Lafayette*, Ind.: Kappa Delta Pi, 1968.

———, *The Slow Learner in the Classroom.* Columbus, Ohio: Charles E. Merrill Books, 1960.

Kidd, J. W., "Toward a More Precise Definition of Mental Retardation." *Ment. Retard.*, Vol. 2, 1964, pp. 202–212.

Kirk, S. A. & Johnson, G. O., *Educating the Retarded Child.* Boston: Houghton Mifflin Co., 1951.

Kolstoe, O. P., & Frey, R. M., *A High School Work-Study Program for Mentally Sub-normal Students.* Carbondale, Ill.: S. Illinois Univ., 1965.

O'Connor, N., & Tizard, J., *The Social Problem of Mental Deficiency.* London, New York: Pergamon Press, 1956.

The President's Panel on Mental Retardation, *A Proposed Program for National Action to Combat Mental Retardation.* Washington: U.S. Govt. Printing Office, 1962, 201 pp.

The President's Committee on Mental Retardation, *MR 67: A first report to the President on the nation's progress and remaining great needs in the campaign to combat mental retardation.* Washington: U.S. Govt. Printing Office, 1967, 32 pp.

Roach, E. G., & Kephart, N. C., *Academic Readiness for the Mentally Retarded Child.* Indianapolis: Indiana Dept. of Mental Health, Division of Special Education, 1962, 28 pp.

———, *The Purdue Perceptual-Motor Survey.* Columbus, Ohio: Charles E. Merrill Books, 1966.

Sloan, W., & Birch, J. W., "A Rationale for Degrees of Retardation." *Amer. J. Ment. Defic.*, Vol. 60, 1955, pp. 258–264.

Strauss, A. A., & Lehtinen, L., *Psychopathology and Education of the Brain-Injured Child.* New York: Grune and Stratton, 1947.

Telford, C. W., & Sawrey, J. B., *The Exceptional Individual.* Englewood Cliffs, N.J.: Prentice-Hall, 1967.

Tilton, James R., *Role of the Center and Proposed Program, Staffing and Budget for 1968.* Lafayette, Indiana. Locally distributed by Wabash Center for the Mentally Retarded, August 1967, 7 pp.

Tredgold, A. F., *A Textbook of Mental Deficiency* (6th ed.). New York: William Wood, 1937.

U.S. Civil Service Commission, *Employment of the Mentally Retarded in Federal Service.* Washington: U.S. Civil Service Comm. (BRI 80–51), April, 1966, 4 pp.

U.S. Department of Health, Education and Welfare Committee on Mental Retardation, *Mental Retardation: Activities of the U.S. Dept. of Health Education and Welfare.* Washington: U.S. Govt. Printing Office, 1962, 77 pp.

Woods, L. C., *Implementing Programs for Educable Mentally Retarded and Other Educationally Handicapped Youth: Work-Oriented Program at the Secondary School Level.* Indianapolis: Ind. Department of Public Instruction, Division of Special Education, 1968, 44 pp.

Younie, W. J., ed., *Guidelines for Establishing School Work-Study Programs for Educable Mentally Retarded Youth.* Richmond, Va.: State Dept. of Education, Special Education Service, 1965, 70 pp.

INDEX